PRESENT PERFECT

Present Perfect Press
Melton Mowbray, UK
2021
All extracts are sourced from texts in the public domain
This publication has no official affiliation
© Jonathan Martin 2021

CIE IGCSE ENGLISH LITERATURE

A guide for scoring top marks in the exams

Contents

A NOTE ON HOW TO USE THIS BOOK

Students taking the CIE IGCSE-level English literature exams will be required to write essay-style answers, and the guidance in this book is tailored toward writing those essays effectively.

Whilst I hope this book will help anyone taking an English literature with any exam board, it is specifically written with the IGCSE syllabus in mind.

The book is designed to be read in its entirety, but it's only a third of the first "Harry Potter" book's length. I know how little spare time GCSE students have.

The most important section to read is Part One, which is all about the approaches and techniques involved in the exam.

Part Two guides you through example essays for the different exam sections. Although these use specific texts, they focus on the techniques you should use no matter what text your class has been studying. So don't worry if I use a text different to yours.

Part Three is an appendix and includes sections on terminology and a bit more on techniques.

PART ONE: EXAM APPROACHES

WHAT IS THE POINT OF AN ESSAY?

Writing a great essay is like writing a great story.

When we write a story, there's a clear purpose: to entertain our readers. We can do this effectively by using strategies such as creating suspense to keep them hooked, throwing in a surprising twist at the climax, and so on. We know the purpose, and therefore we can find good ways to fulfil it.

Imagine writing a story if you didn't understand its purpose was to entertain. It probably wouldn't be very good.

One of the big difficulties with writing essays is not understanding the purpose of them. If you don't know the purpose of your writing, then how can you know what strategies make an effective essay? You have to understand the purpose first.

The purpose is this: an essay is an argument. Your argument. A very similar argument to those good-natured ones you have with family and friends, except this one's in written form.

Think about the purpose of an argument. You have an idea about something, and you justify to other people that your argument is correct. Your idea might be to go to a restaurant in the evening, when your friends would prefer to go to the cinema. You justify this idea with well-considered reasons: the restaurant will be more sociable; it won't take up so much time; you'll all get some good nutrients for your cash rather than wasting it on an unsatisfying film; etc.

It's exactly the same in a literature essay. In the exam, you're given a question: it might be about how a character's portrayed, or what a writer's saying about a certain theme. The examiners want to see your idea in response to this question, and then they want to see you justify that idea with effective analysis of the text.

Having ideas is what this subject is all about. English teachers always say "there's no right or wrong answer in this subject" because it is your own personal idea that's needed. You prove your idea is "right" by justifying it in the main body of your essay.

Key points:

- o An essay is all about having an idea and justifying our idea.
- o Don't worry about what "correct" idea the examiners might expect; instead, feel confident about shaping your own, personal idea – that's what they want to see.

HOW IS AN ENGLISH-LITERATURE ESSAY SPECIAL?

Students quite often approach their literature essays in a similar way to other subjects – especially history. But there is a crucial difference to understand.

In other subjects, essays tend to involve this process:

- o You are given an essay question.
- o You begin by giving some background about the topic and perhaps explaining the process you will use.
- o In your main paragraphs, you analyse sources or experiments.
- o Finally, in your conclusion, you present the answer to the essay question.

This leads to problems in English. Students might follow a similar approach, and not actually give an answer to the essay question until the end. Quite often, introductions will give both sides of an argument, and the student's decision about which side to take isn't revealed until the end.

But this isn't an effective approach to a literature essay, and it's not what the examiners are looking for.

In literature essays, it's vital that we answer the question straight away. The introduction of your essay should give a clear answer to the question. This answer is your personal idea. Your main paragraphs' job is to prove why that answer is correct. The conclusion reinforces your answer.

Key points:

- o Don't try to structure your literature essays in the same way as you would for a history, science, or any other subject's essay.
- o You need to understand the specifics of how to structure a literature essay. This book will help you; your teacher will too.

- Always give a clear answer to the question in your introduction. Be confident – keep your answer hidden away until the conclusion.

VITAL INGREDIENTS OF A TOP-SCORING ESSAY

There are all sorts of things a really good essay needs to be doing, and this book will take you through them all. For now, let's begin with a couple of quite general but very important elements of a top-notch essay.

1) The Conceptual Focus

Writing with a conceptual focus is a hugely powerful thing, and can be a great help in lifting your essays from the 'C' (or 4) to the 'A+' (or 7+) range. So let's look carefully at what a conceptual focus is.

If you're writing conceptually, then you're focusing on the concepts – or ideas – that the writer is communicating.

This is very different to, and much more effective than, simply writing about the characters or plot. A conceptual essay-writer will always think of the characters and plot as devices, or constructs, created by the writer in order to convey deeper ideas.

In essays that don't do this conceptual writing, it tends to seem as if the essayist is writing about **C**haracters **A**s **R**eal **P**eople – this is what I call 'CARPing'. CARPers only think about the characters, how they behave, what they do, etc. CARPers don't tend to think about the writer very much. When you CARP, you never achieve such deep and insightful analysis as when you write conceptually.

Looking at examples can help clarify the difference:

CARPing: *Macbeth is a really evil character in the play. He even goes so far as to have his best friend Banquo killed.*

CONCEPTUAL: *Shakespeare uses Macbeth's assassination of Banquo to show how low a person's morality can sink when influenced by uncontrolled ambition.*

In that example, the CARPer shows she or he possesses some knowledge of the text (AO1), but won't get credit for anything else.

10

The conceptual writer, however, shows deeper understanding of the writer's ideas (AO2) as well as knowledge of the text (AO1). More importantly, the conceptual writer is using an analytical approach – he or she is considering what ideas the writer (Shakespeare) is using the character (Macbeth) to convey.

Achieving a conceptual focus is not difficult. It's all about THINKING and PHRASING. When you're writing about a character or plot event, THINK about what idea the writer is conveying with that character or event. When you're writing the sentence in your essay, PHRASE it so the sentence begins with the writer rather than the character (as in the example above).

A CONCEPTUAL ESSAY-WRITER WILL:

- o   Think about the writer before the characters.
- o   Write about the ideas the writer is conveying through the characters and plot.
- o   Think of, and write about, the characters and plot as devices created by to writer.
- o   Frequently start sentences with the writer's name.
- o   Not worry about whether the writer really intended to convey a deeper idea/concept or not, but just assume that he or she did intend to do so.

2) The Analytical Focus

The second vital ingredient of top-scoring essays is writing with an analytical focus.

By far the most common feedback students receive for their practice essays is that their writing is not analytical enough. They're not analysing enough. If only their essays were more analytical, they'd be scoring great marks. It's just one thing, but it's a big thing, and it's really hard to understand what analytical writing actually is. So let's take a look.

"Analysis" can mean a whole range of different things. If you look up a dictionary definition of "analysis", you'll probably find something along the lines of "a detailed examination" or "a detailed study of something". That's not a very useful definition for us.

In literature essays, it's important to understand that "analysing" means examining how a writer's use of language, structure and form creates meaning and effects. In our essays, although we should try to analyse form and structure too, the bulk of our analysis will be of language. We are simply explaining **how language works** when we analyse.

Our essays have to show we understand the ideas writers communicate in the exam texts, but also that we understand *how* the writer communicates those ideas – how the language (and structure and form) is used by the writer to convey particular ideas and effects. That's what analysis is for.

Describing versus analysing

Two people – Jack and Jill – go to the pub, and they both order a crab sandwich.

Jack bites into his and says, "Ooh, delicious! It really tastes lovely! Very fresh and a nice juicy texture."

Jill bites into hers and says, "Hmm, delicious indeed! I can taste a bit of chilli spice that the chef's put in the mayonnaise, which helps add liveliness to the otherwise subtle flavour of the crab meat. Also, the chef's added just the right amount of lemon juice, which is what makes it taste so fresh."

While Jack's just describing what the sandwich tastes like, Jill is analysing *how it's been made to taste that way.*

The equivalent happens in essays. Many candidates just describe a character...e.g. he's nice. The analysist will examine *how the writer has made the character seem nice.*

No one wants to go to the pub and listen to someone like Jill banging on about her sandwich, but this does hint at how valuable a skill analysis is, and why it's trained in school. Jill's got a deeper understanding of her sandwich. She can go off and make it herself, or start her own sandwich business, etc...

EXAMPLE (of writing with an analytical focus)

Let's use the opening line of William Wordsworth's famous poem:

I wandered lonely as a cloud

The concept here is pretty clear – Wordsworth's conveying an idea about loneliness, but it doesn't sound like a really terrible loneliness. It's not as if the speaker's crying because he's got no friends; instead, it feels as if he is quite contented. The poem's opening concept seems to be more about the happiness, even freedom, of being alone – rather than the torment of it.

So now we've interpreted the concept, we can go on to analyse how the writer uses language to convey the idea of a pleasant loneliness. We could write about the simile comparing the speaker to a cloud – something light and carefree. The image of a cloud by itself implies a clear, blue sky surrounding it, which adds to the cheerful positivity of this loneliness. We could develop analysis by commenting on another detail – the diction of "wandered". This has connotations (associations) of pleasant aimlessness – you might "wander" through your local town centre just enjoying the sights and sounds without having any clear purpose. It helps make the speaker sound as if he's enjoying his loneliness.

And there we have it – that's how we analyse. In that example, I analysed how the writer uses language to convey a concept. We can also analyse how writers portray their characters, how particular feelings or moods are created, and how impact on a reader or audience is created.

A really useful thing to bear in mind when analysing is that you're not analysing a text – you're analysing the writer, and more specifically the writer's methods.

AN ANALYTICAL WRITER WILL:

- o Think about how the text they're writing about works. How the words in it (and the structure and form) are used by the writer to convey particular ideas, feelings, or effects.
- o Think about the text as a construct of the writer – for example, the analytical writer will treat characters as if they are devices created by the writer, not as if they are real people.
- o Understand the difference between interpretation and analysis, and use both skills when writing essays.

HOW THE EXAMS WORK (IGCSE)

The IGCSE Literature in English exams all involve the same fundamental approach: you are given an exam question, and have forty-five minutes (one hour and fifteen minutes in the unseen) to write an essay-style answer.

All candidates will take Paper 1 (Prose and Poetry). This comprises two questions, one on a prose text (novel) you have been studying, and one on a poem you have studied. For the prose section, you can choose to answer a whole-text question OR an extract question. For poetry, you choose one of two poem questions.

This is a closed text exam, so you can't have your copy of the novel with you. However, the poems will be printed in the exam paper.

As well as the Paper 1 exam, you will also be taking ONE of the following:

- o   Paper 2 (Drama; 1.5 hours, closed text). Two essay questions on two plays you have been studying. You MUST do one extract question and one whole-text question – so if, for example, you pick the whole-text question on the first play, then you have to do the extract question for the second play.
- o   Paper 3 (Drama, 45 minutes, open text, one essay question on a play you've studied, choice of whole-text or extract) AND Paper 4 (unseen, 45 minutes).
- o   Paper 3 (same as above) AND component 5 – coursework.

NB: the above is correct at time of writing, but the syllabus may have changed since.

If you've started your IGCSE course (i.e. if you've started Year 10) you should know which of those options you'll be taking, but just ask your teacher if you're not sure.

All the assessment routes involve the same sort of essay-writing task, and they're all marked with the same criteria, which we'll look at in the next section.

HOW EXAM ESSAYS ARE MARKED

It's quite likely your teacher will have given you a copy of the IGCSE literature mark scheme – it's a one-page table with eight 'bands' on it (appearing as rows) over which are split the twenty-five marks you can score for each exam essay.

You may have done a bit of work with this mark scheme; you may have used it to mark your own or others' essays; your teacher may have talked you through it; or, you may never have seen it. Don't worry. They are notoriously tricky to interpret and mark with – but they work.

Your teachers will have used it to mark hundreds, if not thousands, of student essays; they will have moderated their use of the mark scheme against other teachers in your school (and against other schools), and they will have a good understanding of what standard of writing is required in order to hit certain marks on the scheme. Your teachers will also have seen what IGCSE grades are awarded over several years and therefore will have some sense of what mark you need to earn particular grades (but, as your teacher will have said, these 'grade boundaries' can and do change each year).

It therefore takes many years of experience to fully understand how this mark scheme really works, and you haven't got that much time! This section will explain it all to you much more quickly.

Before we talk about what numbers you need to be hitting, let's make sure we understand the structure of the mark scheme and each of its specific objectives.

The mark scheme is split into four different assessment objectives, or 'AOs': AO1, AO2, AO3 and AO4. The examiner will consider how well your essay does with regard to each of these assessment objectives, and come to an overall decision as to where your answer falls on the mark scheme. For example, you might do AO1 and AO2 really well – perhaps hitting band 6 – but you're not so hot on AO3 and AO4 – these are only band 4 quality – therefore, your answer would have a 'best fit' in band 5. Let's see what each AO asks for:

AO1 (knowledge, quotations, writing)

This assessment objective measures your knowledge of the text you're writing about. If you can show you know the whole text well, you'll score highly here. The examiner will be looking for accurate and wide-ranging knowledge of plot and character, but will also be looking for your use of quotations. Using a good range of quotations helps a lot here. Furthermore, **how** you use those quotations is important for AO1 – you need to be integrating them skilfully into your sentences, and we'll look at how to do that later in the book.

Your use of technical terminology influences AO1.

Finally, the style of your writing also helps with AO1. Well-articulated and technically accurate writing is needed to score highly.

AO2 (understanding)

Whereas AO1 assesses your knowledge of a text, AO2 is more interested in how well you understand the text. It's worth thinking about the difference: for example, I can *know* that Macbeth has his friend Banquo killed in Shakespeare's play, but do I *understand* why Macbeth does this?

To do decently well with AO2, you'll need to show at the very least a **surface-level understanding** - e.g. understanding why Banquo is killed, why Lady Macbeth goes mad at the end of the play, why Macbeth's going around killing people, etc.

To earn better marks for AO2, you need to show understanding of the text's **deeper implications**. This is a phrase you'll see in bands 5 and 6 of the mark scheme, and generally it can be understood to mean the text's themes (or 'ideas', or 'concepts'). The destructive nature of unrestrained ambition and the nature of good leadership are themes seen in 'Macbeth'.

The top marks for AO2 go to students who show a **critical understanding** of the text; this phrase appears in the top two bands of the mark scheme. A 'critical understanding' means that, as well as showing surface-level and deeper understanding, you're also thinking about the writer and his or her intentions. To get here, you're no longer just saying "well, this is a play that shows uncontrolled ambition can be dangerous", instead, you're thinking "okay, Shakespeare wants to show his audience how uncontrolled ambition can be really dangerous and these are the ways he does it...". This is why the focus on the writer, which I mentioned before, is so important. A critical understanding will engage with the *why* element. Why does Shakespeare show Lady Macbeth going mad at the end? Well, to show how uncontrolled ambition can be destructive to the self as well as others. *Why* does Shakespeare want to show his audience that this ambition is destructive? Well, because at its heart his play has a theological message about the danger of human ambition interposing into Godly jurisprudence.

That kind of critical understanding leads to a deeper essay which is focused on the writer and the writers intentions, but it can be really hard to sustain.

AO3 (analysis)

You get AO3 credit by analysing the writer's use of language, structure and form.

It is possible to gain some marks just by making very general comments about what the writer is doing. For example, you might be able to explain that a character is portrayed to be cruel, or a setting is made to seem unpleasant, and support your points with appropriate quotations. This will get you some AO3 credit, and will stop your exam essay from being a complete flop.

However, in order to get good marks, you need to be analysing details properly. This means writing about specific words and devices used by the writer, and explaining what effect they create. If you do this convincingly, you'll be able to hit 14-15 out of 25 (as long as you're doing all right with the other AOs too). If your analysis isn't convincing – you haven't explained it well enough, or it doesn't make sense – then you still might not hit these marks.

In order to gain access to the 16-and-upwards range, we need to be doing **developed** and **detailed** analysis. This means commenting on more than one feature of each quotation you're using, and explaining fully how effects are created. We'll look at how to do this later on. AO3 credit will depend upon how consistently developed your analysis is, and how perceptive, interesting, and convincing it is.

Analysing structure and form also gain credit here; it's important to cover these two if you're shooing for the higher marks. Again, we'll look at these later on.

AO4 (personal response)

AO4's an interesting one because it's quite unique to this exam board; not many others ask for it explicitly.

For AO4, the examiner is looking for a sense of your personal connection with the text you're writing about. The examiner wants to see that you have really thought about it, that your ideas are very much your own, and also that you're sensitive to the impact the text has on you as a reader.

This is important, and I think it's good that the exam board asks for it, because all the analysis can get a bit dry and clinical. AO4 encourages us to think about the more emotional impact of the text.

A good sense of personal engagement is therefore necessary for earning good AO4 credit; this assessment objective also asks for 'developed' responses at the higher bands. If your answer isn't very long, it may lose marks against AO4 – and AO3, which also asks for 'development'. See the 'How long should my essay be?' section for more on length.

HOW MANY MARKS YOU NEED TO GET

Now we understand what the mark scheme is asking us to do with its four assessment objectives, let's look more precisely at ow high up the mark scheme we need to be shooting for top marks.

English is not one of those subjects where you have to be getting 90%+ to earn the highest grades. It is a very demanding mark scheme, and it gets incredibly difficult to access the highest bands. But that's okay, because most of the action kicks off around the half-way point of the mark scheme.

So how many marks do we need in order to score an A*, or an 8/9?

First, it's important to stress that it's impossible to guarantee any answer to that question. Every year the grade boundaries change. However, this is what my years of experience with the exam board have shown (starting with letter grades):

There tends to be more of a gap between the 'D'-to-'B' grades than the 'B'-to-'A*' grades, and those lower grades, I think, are less predictable. But a 'C' grade tends to be around the 11/25 mark. (Remember, all exam essays are marked out of 25.) So, if **on average across all your literature exam essays** you scored 11/25, you'd *likely* earn a 'C'.

The 'B' grade averages out at 13/25, but can sometimes be 12 or sometimes 14.

'A' grades tend to fall at 14-15/25. 14 is quite commonly an 'A' grade, but not always.

For the 'A*' – sometimes, 15/25 is enough, but normally 16/25 is a more common 'A*' level. However, 17 is much more secure. When I'm marking my own students' practice papers, I only consider 17/25 to be a secure 'A*' grade.

Remember these numbers are averages for all your exam essays. Unless you're doing the coursework option, you'll be writing a total of four exam essays. If you do two cracking ones that both earn a 17, and two shoddy ones that only get 10 each, that's an average of 13.5 which would work out at an overall literature grade of a high 'B', and possibly an 'A' depending on where the grade boundaries fall that year.

In terms of number grades (9-1) – this is harder to predict because we've got fewer previous years to go on. However, based on current data, it seems to work out roughly the same. So:

Grade 6 = 12/25.

Grade 7 = 14/25.

Grade 8 = 16-17/25.

Grade 9 = 17+/25.

Remember, **these are only estimates**.

The '9' is particularly hard to predict, because the exam board take a certain proportion of the top-scoring candidates and award them the '9'. For example, one year it might be the top 10%; another year the top 8%.

In all honestly, the above information (or prediction) isn't really that useful. It might help to gauge what kind of grade your practice essays are at when your teacher marks them, but do bear in mind that no matter how hard teachers try, our marking won't necessarily be quite the same as examiners'.

What's far more useful is to have an understanding of the quality of essay-writing that's indicative of top-grade answers, so we'll look at that now.

MEETING THE DEMANDS OF THE ASSESSMENT OBJECTIVES

Let's take each AO and look at the quality required for a top-grade response.

AO1 (knowledge, quotations, writing)

AO1's demand that you show knowledge of the text tends to help out weaker candidates. If you can show that you have some knowledge of what happens in the plot and who the characters are, you'll get a bit of AO1 credit – even if you don't get much for the other AOs.

Higher-level essays will show implicit textual knowledge through the strength of their analysis and conceptual engagement – you won't need to worry about making it obvious that you actually know the text. Just try not to make clumsy mistakes such as misspelling the writer's name, or referring to a play as a 'novel' or 'book', etc.

Having said that, it is important that you show you have knowledge of the whole text. If you're writing an essay for a whole-text question, make sure you use a good range of examples from across the text – don't just write about the start of the story. In extract questions, you've got to show you know more of the text than just the extract, so making wider links is really important (more on that in the 'extract' section). In poetry essays, you've got to try and cover the poem as widely as possible.

A really important thing for top-grade AO1 credit is your use of quotations. Quantity is important. In a whole-text question, I recommend aiming to use three quotations in each of your main paragraphs. These should be good quotations which you can use for developed analysis. In extract and poetry tasks, you should use more. This is because you have the printed text in front of you during the exam, so there's an expectation that quotations are easier to find and use.

The way you use these quotations is also really important. They need to be properly integrated into your sentences (your teacher might use the word 'blended', or 'embedded' instead of 'integrated'). We will look at how to do this later in the book, and it's a skill you will work on at some point during your IGCSE course, but always ask your teacher if you're not comfortable with how to do it.

You also need to be writing accurately. Properly structured sentences, a good degree of spelling accuracy (doesn't have to be perfect, but as close to perfect as you can manage), and an appropriately academic tone are all needed to score the highest grades.

AO2 (understanding)

To get to the sweet spot on the mark scheme with AO2, we need to be consistently engaging with the writer's concepts (which means the themes/ideas). This is fairly easy to do with a bit of practice. Just make sure than in every paragraph (including the intro and conclusion) you are giving your thoughts on the writer's intentions.

Example: we're writing an essay in response to this whole-text question: "How does Steinbeck make the relationship between George and Lennie so powerful in 'Of Mice and Men'?" (Don't worry if you don't know the story).

In my intro I'm setting out the argument that the relationship is made to be powerful because it is built on mutual dependency – both George and Lennie need each other for different reasons (Lennie needs George's father-like guidance; George needs Lennie's companionship).</p

I hit AO2 in the intro by explaining that Steinbeck (the author) portrays this mutual dependency in order to highlight how societal circumstances can make life really difficult for people, and forces them to rely on others rather than just themselves. I could also write about how "Of Mice and Men" was set during the Great Depression in America, and it's this tough societal context that Steinbeck is reflecting.

My first main paragraph focuses on how Steinbeck powerfully portrays George's need for companionship, and how Lennie's presence serves as a cure for George's loneliness. I hit AO2 by writing about Steinbeck's intentions – I think Steinbeck is using the characters' bond to show how strong relationships were vital to counter the kind of intense loneliness caused by harsh societal conditions (such as those of the novel's Great-Depression context); none of the other characters have a relationship like George and Lennie's, and they all suffer various forms of intense loneliness.

It feels quite similar to the AO2 point I gave in my introduction – which is good. It means my essay will build a cohesive argument about the writer's deeper ideas and intentions, all linking back to the impact of societal conditions on people (in this example). I keep doing it in my subsequent main paragraphs, and reinforce what I think Steinbeck's saying about "relationships" in the conclusion.

It's important to feel confident when making these AO2 points. Don't get bogged down by doubts such as "what if this isn't what the writer was thinking?". It doesn't matter – all that counts is **your own interpretation of the writer's deeper ideas.**

Some students can weave this conceptual engagement of deeper ideas together with textual analysis, and those tend to be the sort of answers that can get 20+ out of 25 (worth bearing in mind if you're shooting for a '9'). But so long as you're hitting AO2 in each paragraph (including intro and conclusion), and you're giving well-considered thoughts, you'll be doing enough to score top grades.

Finally for AO2 – I've got one secret weapon that can be really helpful, and it's the "ITTIRA" sentence.

"ITTIRA" stands for '**I t**hink **t**his _____ **i**s **r**eally **a**bout'. You fill in the blank with 'novel', or 'play', or 'poem', depending on what sort of text you're writing about.

It's a great, quick way of showing you've got a deep understanding of the whole text – really helpful for AO2 credit. I like to whip it out in the conclusion, and all I have to do is link it to the exam task. Take for an example the same 'Of Mice and Men' question I used above. In my conclusion, I'll write something like this.:

*I think this novel is really about **the heavy impact societal circumstances have on people's personal lives**, and Steinbeck uses the destruction of George and Lennie's relationship to portray this impact in a powerfully poignant fashion.*

The emboldened phrase is one I can have prepared before the exam for whatever text I'm going to be writing about. After that, I simply link it to the exam task. Easy to do, and your examiner will love it.

AO3 (analysis)

The main thing to say here is that in order to earn top grades we must be analysing properly. A lot of students don't do this, and it's certainly the most common reason people get held back from 'A' and '7+' grades.

Top-grade analysis means "developed" analysis. You'll see this word in the mark scheme in band 6, where the 'A*' grade tends to fall. We've already looked at an example of developed analysis, and we'll look at more later in the book. Essentially it means we're writing in detail about how writers create meaning/effect. We're not just giving one quick comment about a simile we've spotted, we're instead exploring in careful detail how the writer has used that simile. When we use a key quotation, we don't just write about one thing in it – we pick at least two features of the quotation to comment on.

Furthermore, top-grade analysis won't restrict itself to analysis of language – it will analyse structure and form as well. Don't panic if you're not sure what 'structure' and/or 'form' means – there's a section later in this book that will help you.

AO4 (personal response)

This is probably the hardest AO to qualify in terms of top-grade standard. It's going to depend a lot on your natural skill.

To award top-grade credit for AO4, the examiner needs to feel that you're giving your own ideas – and that you're exploring them. If you've relied heavily on, for example, online study guides to learn about the exam texts, and in your exam essay you use a lot of those ideas, it's likely the examiner won't feel convinced that you're giving your own thoughts.

You can help this along by signposting your personal engagement. Using phrases such as "I think...", "I feel..." etc. is **good** for this exam board (because of AO4). Include yourself in your essay – write about **your** thoughts, about what the text/characters make you feel, and about the impact of the text on you. It's possible you might have been taught not to use "I think..." in essays, perhaps even when you were back in primary school, but it is something good to do for this particular exam board.

Looking at examples of personal engagement is a good way to get a feel for it, so the examples in this book should help.

Top-grade AO4 credit also relies on "development", so the length of your answer is important. Remember: three main paragraphs along with an introduction and a conclusion (so five paragraphs in total) is a good target. When practising, I advise my students to aim for three sides of lined A4 – based on average handwriting size.

This section has given us quite a lot to digest, so let's summarise it here:

AO1

- o   Use three good, integrated quotations in main paragraphs (more in extract or poetry essays).

- o Aim for wide coverage of the text – take quotations from across the novel/play/poem; use a range of characters where appropriate (some questions ask about one character).

AO2

- o Target AO2 in every paragraph – comment on the writer's intention/deeper idea.
- o Use an ITTIRA sentence (conclusions or intros are best for this).

AO3

- o Give developed analysis of all quotations in your main paragraphs.
- o Give analysis of structure and form at some point in your answer.

AO4

- o Signpost your personal engagement with "I think…" phrases.
- o Aim to write 2-3 sides of lined A4 (which is more like 3-4 sides of an exam answer booklet).

HOW LONG SHOULD MY ESSAY BE?

There are a few things to bear in mind here, but a straightforward answer would be two to three sides of lined A4. You'll do most of your practice on lined A4, but you'll find in exams, answer booklets have less space to write on each page so four sides is better to aim for. By that point, you'll have a good feel for how long your essay needs to be (provided you've been practising!).

The mark scheme asks for developed responses, so it's quite clear that you can't get the highest grades if your answer is too short – no matter how amazing your analysis might be.

However, it's not just a matter of simple length – your essay should also cover a good range of topics, and should cover the text well. If you're writing about a poem, you need to try and use details from all stanzas; if you're writing about a novel or play, use details from the beginning, middle and end of the story.

Three main paragraphs, each with a sharp focus on a specific topic, along with an introduction and conclusion normally satisfies these demands. You'll be able to give developed paragraphs, and three is enough for a range of topics. It won't be easy – the forty-five minute time limit will be a real push. Practice in strict timed conditions is therefore really important.

PART TWO: EXAMPLE ESSAYS

1) DRAMA, WHOLE TEXT

The previous sections should have given some sense of what an essay is, and what the mark scheme requires. Let's now put all this into practice by taking an exam question and working through a full answer.

We'll use 'Macbeth' – it's often on the IGCSE syllabus and is a popular choice among schools. But don't worry if you're not doing it – it's the techniques and approach that we need to learn here. When you've got a better understanding of those, you can use them with your own exam texts.

Nevertheless, you might like a quick plot summary of Shakespeare's play if you don't know it. But it's not important, so feel free to skip over this if you want!

'Macbeth' is about a Scottish lord (called Macbeth) in the Middle Ages who meets some witches (yes – proper old-school witches who cackle, make spells, etc.). They tell him he'll become 'Thane of Cawdor' (a promotion) and then King of Scotland (an even better promotion). Immediately, Macbeth starts to imagine murdering the current king to help make this prophecy come true, but he only daydreams about doing so. It's his wife, Lady Macbeth, who compels him to go through with this this terrible act.

So Macbeth murders Duncan, who everyone loved, and becomes King of Scotland. But he's paranoid – everything seems like a threat to his new position; even his best friend Banquo seems to be a danger. Because the witches said that Banquo's children would one day become Kings/Queens, Macbeth sees this as a threat to his own line – so he has his friend assassinated. He also intended for Banquo's son to be killed, but the boy escapes.

Macbeth starts to struggle with the guilt of the terrible things he's done. People start to notice his strange behaviour, especially when he sees Banquo's ghost at one of his royal parties. Desperate to keep his throne secure, Macbeth asks for advice from the witches and decides to go on with the killings. The wife and child of Macduff, another Scottish lord (who Macbeth doesn't like), are next to be assassinated by Macbeth's dogsbodies.

The Scottish people soon get pretty sick of Macbeth's tyrannical behaviour, and they team up with an English army to overthrow Macbeth. The final act of the play sees Lady Macbeth going mad with guilt, and Macbeth becoming increasingly wild in his determination to keep his crown. After much nastiness, Macduff kills Macbeth, and the Scottish throne is taken by Malcolm, Duncan's son and rightful heir.

It's a play with concepts (themes/ideas) such as the dangerous nature of uncontrolled ambition, the nature of bad and good leadership (Macbeth vs Malcolm), and the conflict between fate and free will.

EXAM QUESTION: To what extent do you believe Macbeth is a powerful character?

This is the kind of question exam boards like, because it helps to differentiate good students from weaker ones. Most students will be able to write about Macbeth being powerful in the way he becomes king and holds on to his position with an often violent determination. But stronger students will be able to tackle the complexities, such as:

- o Macbeth's lack of free will makes him powerless: his actions are determined by greater, ethereal forces embodied in the three witches, and by his wife.
- o The dichotomy (difference/conflict) between Macbeth's martial power and moral power. 'Martial' refers to fighting and war – so whilst Macbeth is a brave soldier at the start of

31

the play and a powerful, vicious tyrant at the end, his morality is lacking in power/strength and is easily overridden by his ambition.

So – good candidates, such as yourself, should immediately be looking for complexities when they see the exam question. Your ability to do this will be determined by how well you know the text, but mainly by your terrific thinking.

PLANNING AND STRUCTURING

Always plan. I advise a minimal plan – so minimal that it may only take a matter of seconds rather than minutes. Even a barebones plan like this is important for a couple of reasons:

1) It gives you chance to sort out the structure of your essay – and the best essays must have a sense of structure.

2) It shows your examiner that you are thinking about your argument and structure. The examiner will see your plan and realise you are conscious of your essay's organisation.

My barebones plan is very simple: it needs an idea for the essay's **central argument** (also known as a 'thesis') and ideas for how that argument can be broken down over **three main-paragraph topics**.

Okay: let's remind ourselves of the question:

To what extent do you believe Macbeth is a powerful character?

Remember – this is much more about our ideas than our knowledge. We need to know the text, but that knowledge is just a foundation for the really important thing – our argument.

I'll start by writing 'PLAN' on my answer paper and jotting down a few thoughts relevant to the question (Macbeth as a powerful character): *brave soldier, becomes king, takes people's lives, determined to keep his throne, BUT manipulated by witches, persuaded by his wife, visions influence him.*

Simply getting down some nice straightforward points can help us start thinking of a central argument; I'm going to go with:

CENTRAL ARGUMENT: Macbeth is powerful in a martial sense, but much less so in matters of conscience.

("Martial" meaning related to war, fighting, etc.) This is a decently complex argument; it enables me to contrast Macbeth's obvious strength with his morally weak conscience that is easily influenced by other forces.

That's going to be the backbone of my essay, so I write it clearly in my plan and put a big circle around it. At the moment it's not conceptual – the argument is only about the character. So, I'll add a quick comment beneath it:

CONCEPTUALISE: Shakespeare shows us power comes in different types.

It's conceptual, because it's focusing on the writer's deeper idea. It is a bit shallow, but I can flesh it out in my essay and having it noted in my plan will remind me to do so.

Now I just need to think how I can structure this argument, so I'll choose the topics I will use in my three main paragraphs. The central argument can be broken down nicely like this:

- *PARA 1: Macbeth's martial power – Act 1,2,3.* [Here, I'l write about his bravery as a soldier, and his power as a king.]
- *PARA 2: Macbeth influenced by the witches and wife – Act 1,2,4.* [Here I will look at the more complex, "powerless" part of the argument – Macbeth's susceptibility to external forces.]
- *PARA 3: Macbeth's power is ultimately vanquished by morally superior forces – Act 5.*

There we go – we think of a central argument, then simply plan how it can be broken down over three paragraphs, so that each main paragraph analyses a separate aspect of the argument. This is "structuring" an essay.

I put in my plan a brief reference to acts in the play that I can use for quotations – this is mainly to check that I am **covering the whole text**. It's not essential to get every single act into the answer – or every chapter if you're writing about a novel – but it would be a concern if I was only going to be using details from a couple of acts, or just from the beginning/ending.

This is also a good moment to consider the structure of your essay by thinking about how you will sequence your topics. It's best to put them in a logical order, and an order which will show some kind of progression, or development, of ideas.

Here, the order in which I've listed the topics above works nicely – we start in the first main paragraph by looking at the ways Macbeth does have power; the subsequent main paragraphs look at his weaknesses/lack of power. It's straightforward and logical.

At first, it might take a while to note down even a brief plan like that, but with practice – and providing you know the text well – you'll be able to bash it out in no time. A good revision/practice strategy is to look at a list of past-paper questions and just practise planning:

Central argument -> conceptualise -> three main-para topics -> sequence.

INTRODUCTION

The main aim in your introduction is to fully and clearly establish your conceptualised central argument. Remember it's vital in a literature essay that we give a strong, direct answer to the exam question right away – that's what our argument does.

Let's start by looking at a typical introductory paragraph of the sort that a lot of mid-level students write, and see if we can spot what's wrong with it:

(A reminder of the exam task: To what extent do you believe Macbeth is a powerful character?)

<u>INTRO (BAD EXAMPLE):</u> *This play is about the character Macbeth, who is very ambitious and becomes king. Shakespeare uses various language techniques to show that in some ways Macbeth is a powerful character, and in some ways he isn't, for example he is able to become king but also he is controlled by the witches.*

So what's wrong with it? Well – let's look at what's good first. The opening sentence is an "overview sentence" of the whole play, which goes some way to showing the candidate's knowledge of the play – good for AO1. At the end, it mentions some examples from the play, also good for AO1.

Unfortunately, that's about all it's got going for it.

The main issue here is that it doesn't clearly answer the question – there's no clear argument being shaped. This is something that happens a lot, because candidates don't understand how to form an argument (or they don't know that they should be forming an argument in the intro).

It only gives a very vague and general comment about Macbeth being powerful in some ways, but this is no way near specific enough to be a strong argument.

"[The writer] uses language techniques..." quite commonly appears in an intro, but it's a very weak sentence. It's analytical, because it's looking at the writer's method, and therefore belongs in a main paragraph rather than an introduction, where we should be establishing argument rather than analysing. But it's too imprecise to be of any value, even if it were in a main paragraph. It's the same as saying "the writer uses words...".

Enough faffing about – let's see what a good introduction *should* look like:

INTRO (GOOD EXAMPLE): *On the face of it, I'd certainly argue that Macbeth, the eponymous protagonist of Shakespeare's play, is a powerful character. His rise from "valiant" soldier to King of Scotland is a quick and violent one, and sees him shedding the blood of his best friend, the rightful king, and innocent women and children. His power is unquestionable in its tyranny – but not in its morality. I believe Shakespeare is showing us the discrepancy between two types of power – martial power, and the power of the moral conscience. It is the latter where Macbeth seems much weaker, and much more susceptible to the influence of external forces.*

What's good about this? Immediately it establishes quite a personal tone – 'I'd certainly argue' right away suggests a personal response to the text and task, which is so important for AO4. "On the face of it" may sound a bit colloquial (chatty/informal) in tone, but it helps with the sense of personal engagement. The tone is soon made more academic with good literary diction such as "eponymous" (an eponymous character is a character whose name appears in the title of the text: Macbeth, Harry Potter, and Oliver Twist are all eponymous characters).

The description of Macbeth's rise to power is quite vividly conveyed, which helps with the sense that the candidate is engaged with the text (AO4). It also shows knowledge of the text; good for AO1.

Notice that I support argument with a short quotation – this also helps with AO1 (knowledge of the text). However, I have not analysed it, because we only want to be analysing the text in the main paragraphs, not the intro.

There is a clear argument established in response to the question, and it is a conceptualised argument ("I believe Shakespeare is showing us the discrepancy between two types of power...") – really good for AO2, because it's focusing on the concept – or idea – that I feel the writer intends to convey to the audience.

Remember, it doesn't matter if you're not writing about "Macbeth"! The same approach should be used with any text:

o   Give a clear, direct argument in response to the task.
o   Conceptualise your argument.
o   Show knowledge of the text.
o   Show a sense of your personal engagement with the text.

Good. Now we've got a cracking intro, let's move on to the first main paragraph where we start to analyse the text.

MAIN PARAGRAPHS

A reminder of the exam task we're working with: **To what extent do you believe Macbeth is a powerful character?**

Now that we have established our argument in the introduction, we must prove that our argument is correct and valid. It's just as if you're having a debate at home, or in any other context. You state your view (introduction) and then prove that your view is correct (main paragraphs). Here, we prove our argument by analysing the text.

There are three big elements to a main paragraph:

o   The topic intro.
o   Detailed, developed analysis.
o   Conceptual engagement.

In this section, we'll look at each of these three elements separately.

THE TOPIC INTRO

This is the first sentence of our main paragraph. It's a really important one, because it's where we make clear for the examiner what topic this paragraph will focus on.

It's *extremely* noticeable when candidates don't use a topic intro. Their main paragraphs lack any clear focus, and their writing wanders from one topic to another. Starting each main paragraph with a good topic intro helps greatly with the overall structure and clarity of your essay.

They are also very easy to write – especially if you've done the sort of plan suggested earlier in this book.

According to my plan from earlier, Macbeth's martial power is the first topic – or the first part of my central argument I'll be analysing. All I need to do is signpost this in a topic intro.

Let's make it clear, specific, and no longer than it needs to be. Here are some examples of topic intros we could use – which do you think is the best?

1) *Macbeth has power in the martial sense – he begins as a brave soldier and becomes an unrelenting tyrant.*

2) *Shakespeare portrays Macbeth's martial power – the character begins as a brave soldier and becomes an unrelenting tyrant.*

3) *Shakespeare portrays Macbeth's martial power to show that power can come in different forms and is not always good.*

What do you think? They are all acceptable, because they identify a specific topic for the paragraph (martial power). But let's think about which does it the most successfully.

1) Is very much character focused. It's treating Macbeth as a real person rather than a character in a text – not so good.

2) is better because it's got a more analytical approach – it focuses on the writer, and on Macbeth as a device. Good.

3) is the most conceptual – it's engaging with the writer's deeper purpose/idea/message, which is good for AO2.

2) or 3) are the best topic intros to go with, and I tend to aim for ones in the style of 2). It's not so conceptual as 3), but that allows us to build up to a conceptual mini-conclusion for the main paragraph. Sometimes, having a very conceptual topic intro means

sacrificing some character detail, which you can see happening here if you compare 2) and 3) above.

So we'll go with 2) – it focuses on the writer, identifies a specific paragraph topic, and gives us room to build toward a conceptual conclusion for the paragraph.

DETAILED, DEVELOPED ANALYSIS

Now we get into the main meat of the essay, and start targeting AO3: the analysis.

A big, common mistake here, which even clever students make, is not analysing. Often people will use quotations but only in a way that supports their argument – they're not actually analysing. I think that's quite frequently because students don't understand what 'analysing' means. I discussed this in an earlier section, but remember: when we analyse a text, we write about **how** the **playwright/author/poet uses language (words, devices, etc.) to create meaning and effect.**

The specific meaning or effect depends on your paragraph topic. Here, our topic is Macbeth's martial power, so we are analysing how Shakespeare portrays Macbeth's martial power.

Even if "Macbeth" isn't one of your exam texts, this will still be a good model of analytical technique which you can transfer to any essay.

After the topic intro, it's important to move into the analysis quickly so we can start getting AO3 credit. Students sometimes spend too long at the start of the main paragraph discussing their argument and developing it – best to do that toward the end, or blend it with your analysis.

My first analysis of Macbeth's martial power will come from the start of the play, Act 1 Scene 2, where Macbeth's role in a battle is being described by a sergeant. This is before we even meet Macbeth himself. (You don't have to use quotations in the same order as they

39

appear in the text – you can start with quotations from the end of the text if you want.) This is the key quotation I'll use:

> *For brave Macbeth--well he deserves that name--*
> *Disdaining fortune, with his brandish'd steel,*
> *Which smoked with bloody execution,*
> *Like valour's minion carved out his passage*
> *Till he faced the slave*

Blimey; it's a big quotation. I can't just dump the whole thing into my paragraph. We need to handle it properly – the examiners are looking at the actual mechanics of how we use quotations in our writing (AO1). So, we need two really important skills: contextualising and integrating.

"Integrating" means blending the quotation into your sentence, so that the quotation(s) becomes a grammatical component of your sentence. Here is a quotation which **isn't** integrated:

Macbeth's power as a soldier is established by the sergeant's description of Macbeth on the battlefield "his brandished steel which smoked with bloody execution".

And here is one which **is** integrated:

Macbeth's power as a soldier is established through the sergeant's description of his "brandished steel...smoking with bloody execution" on the battlefield.

In the first, bad, example, the quotation is simply tagged on at the end of the sentence. It feels very clunky. The second example successfully integrates the quotation, and uses an ellipsis (...) to omit unnecessary words from the original quotation.

"Contextualising" simply means indicating what part of the text or plot the quotation is taken – it's giving the quotation some context. Let's add some contextualisation now:

Macbeth's power is established early; when the sergeant reports on the battle against Macdonwald in 1.2, he describes Macbeth's "brandished steel...which smoked with bloody execution" on the battlefield.

"1.2" is a way of referencing acts and scenes in plays – here, it means act one scene two. You don't have to reference specific scenes/chapters/pages when contextualising; it is fine just to give a decent sense of whereabouts the quotation comes from.

I'm not quite happy with this yet. It's too character focused; we want to keep the focus on the writer. So let's make a little change:

Shakespeare establishes Macbeth's power early; when the sergeant reports on the battle against Macdonwald in 1.2, he describes Macbeth's "brandished steel...which smoked with bloody execution" on the battlefield.

Lovely. Don't worry if you find yourself repeating the writer's name a lot – it's a good thing, and means you're likely maintaining a nice critical focus.

Now we've introduced a nicely contextualised and integrated quotation, we're ready to start analysing the heck out of it.

We've got to keep in mind the argument we're making (Macbeth is powerful in the martial sense) and focus analysis on how the writer creates this. Look again at the quotation we're using:

"His brandished steel...which smoked with bloody execution".

It's a vivid image of Macbeth, with his sword, cutting up his enemies so that their blood seems like smoke coming from his sword. It's non-literal language, which is imagery, and it uses a metaphor.

Great. But let's beware – a lot of candidates will spot the metaphor of Macbeth's "smoking" sword, write a comment about it, and move on to another quotation. No! That does not make for detailed and developed analysis. Instead, we need to find more things in the same quotation.

We could also comment on individual words and the effect they create (this is looking at the writer's **diction**). What looks important here? "Execution" – it highlights the fact that Macbeth is delivering death, but it also has the connotation of justice. Criminals are executed, so it makes it seem as if Macbeth's killing is done justly, rather than just being barbaric acts of murder.

The diction of "bloody" is simple – it's a straightforward adjective – but it has a lot of power in its simplicity, efficiently conveying the violent destruction wrought by Macbeth's martial power.

When you "brandish" a weapon you do so in readiness for a fight – this diction makes Macbeth seem prepared and bold rather approaching the battle coyly.

Why does Shakespeare refer to Macbeth's "steel" rather than his "sword"? This is a device called a **metonym**, which is when a part of something is used to refer to the whole thing. A common metonym is "wheels". When you see your friend driving a new car, you might say, "Hey, nice wheels." You mean the whole car, not just the wheels – so "wheels" is a metonym for "car".

Here, the steel part of the sword (the blade) is a metonym for the whole sword. "Steel" connotes hardness, determination, danger, and power – and therefore Macbeth's character also becomes associated with these qualities.

Having looked at these specific details, we can also consider what overall, combined effect they have. It seems to me as if they are all serving to highlight Macbeth's powerful heroism in the battle, but almost to the point that it becomes hyperbolic. It is as if Macbeth is elevated to a figure from myth and legend rather than being an actual soldier. The fact that we hear this description from the sergeant's report compounds this effect – we are being told the legend of heroic Macbeth. Suddenly his "power" doesn't seem so reliable, as it's been turned into an element of storytelling rather than reality.

That's a big heap of analytical meat – too big, in fact. Bearing in mind this is only one quotation and I've only got forty-five minutes to write my whole essay, I'm not going to be able to say everything I want. So I'm going to select the best bits and ditch the rest. This is called selecting and rejecting, and it's something normally unavoidable for even the best essay writers when working in timed conditions.

When selecting and rejecting, we need to make sure we keep a good balance of specific language points along with the more complex, argumentative points. We also want a range of analytical approaches – I've found a lot of diction in this quotation, so I'll reject some of it. Here's my full analysis of the first quotation:

Shakespeare establishes Macbeth's power early; when the sergeant reports on the battle against Macdonwald in 1.2, he describes Macbeth's 'brandished steel...which smoked with bloody execution' on the battlefield. The metaphor of Macbeth's sword 'smoking' with mists of blood creates an undeniably powerful impression of the character quite literally tearing through his enemies. It strikes me as quite horrific, but Shakespeare's diction of 'execution' brings a sense of justice to Macbeth's martial power – his enemies, just like criminals, are being justly executed rather than murdered. The metonym of 'steel' shapes impressions of power through its connotations of hardness and danger, attributes which are transferred to Macbeth himself. Overall, there's quite a hyperbolic tone – it seems to me as if Macbeth is being elevated to a figure from myth, an effect compounded by Shakespeare's choice to have this description narrated by the sergeant. The audience is hearing the legend of Macbeth, not the reality, which already brings into question just how real and reliable his power actually is.

Let's play close attention to certain things here. Notice after I introduce the quotation, I keep referring back to details from it, using more integrated quotations. This is good practice; it shows the examiner you are analysing in detail, and it maintains a good frequency of quotations.

The analysis is **developed** - a key thing for getting the highest grades. It's not just that I cover a range of details from the quotation, but I use them to build an overall, quite complex analytical idea about Macbeth becoming a figure of myth.

I make several references to myself within the analysis – I comment on what Shakespeare's language makes me think about. This is great for AO4.

So far so good. I've started building my first main paragraph with developed analysis of a quotation. Now I need to build it further by using at least one more quotation, while staying faithful to the paragraph's topic.

For this topic of Macbeth's martial power I'm going to use details from Act 2, as Macbeth prepares to murder the current king, and from Act 3, when Macbeth's own kingly power is on display. Here follows my continuation of the paragraph – look out for how I handle quotations, analyse language, maintain focus on the writer and embed my personal engagement:

Shakespeare gives another demonstration of Macbeth's strength as the character prepares for the murder of King Duncan in Act 2. At the end of his famous 'dagger' monologue, Macbeth seems to build a powerful confidence, as shown in his declarative statements such as 'I go, and [the murder] is done'. He seems fully committed to the act. However, I think Shakespeare again casts some ambiguity about the true extent of Macbeth's power. When the character says 'the bell invites me', it gives me the impression that Macbeth isn't acting entirely of his own agency, but is being coerced by external forces (the 'bell'). Later, when Macbeth himself takes the throne from the murdered Duncan, initially he strikes a powerful figure – symbolised by the grand banquet held for the Scottish nobility. Shakespeare shows Macbeth commanding his lords to 'sit down' and adopting spoken mannerisms of royalty such as the plural pronoun: 'our self will mingle with society'. But this outward show of strength is immediately undone when he begins hallucinating Banquo's ghost.

You might have noticed that I'm not developing analysis of these quotations so much as I did with the first. I could if there were time, but there's not in the exam. As expert essay writers in timed conditions, we have to balance the amount of development we do with the amount of quotations we cover. Nevertheless, I still make specific analytical comments on details of Shakespeare's language, and on his use of symbolism.

This gives me a paragraph which has one really developed analysis of a quotation, along with more concise analysis that enables me to include wider coverage of quotations from the play. Good balancing.

FINISHING THE MAIN PARAGRAPH

This is one of those tricky moments in an essay – how to neatly finish a main paragraph? It can often feel as if we're leaving a paragraph unfinished, and moving too quickly to the next.

To help with this, we should think of our last sentence (or two) as being a mini conclusion for the paragraph. In this sentence you have one main aim:

Focus on the paragraph topic and explain what you think the writer is saying about it.

This helps you get credit for AO2 (writing about the deeper ideas of the text/writer) and AO4 (your personal engagement with the text). We need to think of something 'deep', whilst making sure our mini conclusion stays relevant to the essay task and our central argument.

Looking back at my example paragraph, it's clear that Shakespeare is showing Macbeth as someone possessing martial power (which was my topic intro). However, it's also clear that Macbeth's power is always undermined by something – made to seem less reliable by aspects of storytelling, or being brought into question by external forces. So what is Shakespeare saying about Macbeth's power, and, more importantly, the nature of power?

Here's my mini conclusion:

Therefore, while Shakespeare does portray Macbeth as possessing martial power, it is a power that is constantly undermined. I think Shakespeare is showing the audience that martial 'power' held by tyrants is something quite superficial, and is often nothing more than a performance to hide the tyrant's weaknesses.

It's important that I go beyond just saying what the writer is showing us about the character. I take it beyond the text, and explain what I think the writer is showing us about something in our real world (the concept of "power"). This really helps with AO2, and the discussion of the text's thematic elements.

I use the task keyword "power" liberally to help maintain sharp relevance to the exam task.

My use of the word "audience" is important – it shows I am aware that the text is a drama, and how the writer is conveying ideas.

It's a big, well-developed paragraph. But it is big. Don't be daunted – keep practising, and you'll be knocking out chunky analytical paragraphs like this in ten minutes (or so).

TRANSITIONING

That's one main paragraph done. For the next, I just look back at my plan, and build another paragraph for the next topic using the same approach.

There's one thing we need to try and do differently in subsequent main paragraphs, and it regards the topic intro. Ideally, our topic intros should give a nice smooth transition from the previous paragraph. This leads to a more cohesive essay than just abruptly switching to a different topic.

My first main paragraph was about Macbeth's martial power. According to my plan, the second main paragraph is more focused on how Macbeth lacks power, and is influenced heavily by his wife and the witches.

Here's what an untransitioned topic intro would look like for the second main paragraph:

Shakespeare shows Macbeth lacking power because he is so heavily influenced by outside forces such as his wife and the witches.

Here's a transitioned one:

Shakespeare raises further issues about the superficiality of power by showing how Macbeth's is heavily undermined by external forces such as his wife and the witches.

This links neatly with what I was writing at the end of the first main paragraph by using a word from it ("superficial"), and introduces my next paragraph topic. It is also conceptual, keeping focus on what Shakespeare is showing us about a thing/concept/idea (power) rather than just a character.

Here is my second main paragraph, written with the same approaches and techniques as demonstrated above for the first. Read it as if you were an examiner, and look where credit can be given for each of the AOs.

Shakespeare raises further issues about the superficiality of power by showing how Macbeth's is heavily undermined by external forces such as his wife and the witches. I find it striking how Shakespeare is very quick to undermine the audience's initial impressions of Macbeth's martial power, which starts to happen in the first few scenes. In act one scene five, Lady Macbeth reads his letter about the witches' prophecy that he will become king. In a soliloquy, she worries that he is "too full of the milk of human kindness" to "catch the nearest way" (meaning to kill the current king and take his place on the throne). Shakespeare plays on the feminine, maternal connotations of "milk" to strip Macbeth of his masculine power. "Too full" implies an unsettling idea that "power" and "kindness" are mutually exclusive. She goes on to wish for Macbeth's return home, so she can "pour [her] spirits in [his] ear" – she plans to exert her own power of persuasion on him. In this metaphorical imagery, Shakespeare makes Macbeth become a mere object, something like a jug that can have liquid "poured" into it. This is a sharp way of conveying Macbeth's lack of power – he is passive rather than active; influenced rather than influencing. I think Shakespeare's staging is really important here. Lady Macbeth is alone on stage and Macbeth is absent, which gives a strong visual cue about who holds power in the relationship. The witches, another feminine entity, also serve to strip Macbeth of power. Banquo describes Macbeth as "rapt" when they first see the witches on the "heath", as if Macbeth is immediately subject to their control. When he visits them again in act four scene one, the witches' power over Macbeth, and his lack of power, is again highlighted by Shakespeare. The witches' conjuring of apparitions such as the "bloody child", the "show of eight kings" etc. feels remarkably theatrical, as if the audience is watching a play within a play. To me it feels orchestrated and contrived, but Macbeth fails to register this and takes the witches in good faith. Shakespeare crafts strong dramatic irony, where the audience can see Macbeth is being tricked but he cannot. In that sense, the audience have more power than Macbeth. Therefore, I think Shakespeare shows us how fragile "power" can be. Macbeth's outward appearance of being powerful is completely undermined by the influence exerted upon him by Lady Macbeth and the witches.

Some points to note: there's not so much analysis of language in this paragraph; instead, I do more analysis of Shakespeare's staging. This is good when writing about a play – analyse how the playwright controls the stage and shapes the drama. I do it here by discussing how the scene with the witches feels as if it's a play within a play, etc.

This paragraph would get good credit for AO2, because I discuss what I think Shakespeare is saying about the concept of power.

I signpost my personal engagement for AO4 with phrases such as "I find it striking", "I think", "to me it feels...". But more importantly for AO4 is the examiner's sense that these ideas are mine – I'm showing my own ideas about the play rather than just repeating what I've heard my teacher say or what I've read in study guides.

I make specific references to act and scene numbers, which isn't obligatory but does help to contextualise whatever part of the play you're writing about and shows your knowledge of the text – good for AO1.

Terminology:

- o <u>Soliloquy</u>: a speech given by a character who is not speaking to anyone directly. Different to a monologue, which is a speech addressed to another character, or to the audience.
- o <u>Dramatic irony</u>: a device where the playwright gives the audience more knowledge than the character on stage. Clear examples come in pantomimes, where you get the "he's behind you!" moments. The audience knows, but the character doesn't. It's good for analysis because it often strongly impacts the audience's impression of the character – e.g. it makes him/her seem a bit dim.

Now I'll go ahead and bash out a third main paragraph, using the topic in my plan above, and then all we need is a conclusion for a full essay answer.

There is something else Shakespeare does which makes me feel the protagonist is not powerful: he makes Macbeth become an immoral character, and gives power to the more moral Scottish rebels whom Macbeth battles against at the end of the play. In defeating Macbeth, the rebels take his martial power, but their moral power is what leads the audience to celebrate their victory and align with them. Shakespeare's structuring of the final act gives me a strong sense of how the rebels' morality juxtaposes, and highlights, Macbeth's lack of morality. The scenes alternate strictly between the rebels and Macbeth. In those with the rebels, we see Malcolm, the rightful king, speaking with compassion and comradeship: "cousins, I hope the days are near at hand that chambers will be safe...I would the friends we miss were safe arrived". He addresses the soldiers he commands as family, rather than by their lower status, and Shakespeare gives him diction that connotes moral integrity such as "safe" and "friends". This juxtaposes sharply with Macbeth's scenes, where calls his servant a "cream-faced loon" and commands him to "go prick thy face". His language lacks moral integrity, being characterised instead by crude, monosyllabic fury. This later manifests in Macbeth's actions as well as his language. When Young Siward bravely confronts the "abhorred tyrant", Macbeth shows no mercy, striking him down with a "smile" and "laugh". Shakespeare's showing the horrified audience a lot about power, here. Whilst Macbeth still has the power of physical force, it has no value without the power of morality. Shakespeare rams this home when Macbeth loses his physical, martial power – emblematised by the image of righteous Macduff exiting the stage "with Macbeth's (dead) body".

Some points to note: with AO3, you get credit for analysing language, but also for analysing the structure and form of the text. Here, I analyse how Shakespeare's structuring of act five's scenes has impact, which is great for AO3.

Again, I'm exploring new, deeper ideas about the task keyword "power", and discussing what I think Shakespeare is saying about it in the play.

Terminology:

Monosyllabic language: this means words that only have one ("mono") syllable. Macbeth uses a lot of monosyllabism in act five. A character who speaks with heavy monosyllabism can come across as crude, rough, or simplistic (or sometimes confident and bold, depending on the context). I could possibly develop analysis a bit when I mention it, by discussing how the monosyllabism makes Macbeth seem more harsh and aggressive than Malcolm.

CONCLUSION

The most difficult thing about writing conclusions is finding the time. We've written three chunky, developed main paragraphs and may have very little time left in the exam.

If you find you have absolutely no time left to write a conclusion, don't panic about it. Credit for the assessment objectives comes mainly from your intro and (especially) your main paragraphs. If you've done a good job with the intro, the conclusion becomes less vital.

However, a concise conclusion is good to add, because it cements the cohesive structure of your essay, and that is it's job. The conclusion should give a final reinforcement of **your argument**, leaving your examiner with a clear, concise impression of how you are answering the essay task.

Therefore, a conclusion can simply repeat the argument you gave in your introduction. Try not to write it in exactly the same words as you did in the intro, but giving the same argument again gives your essay that nice sandwich-like structure it should have.

For an example, we should first look back at what we wrote in the intro:

On the face of it, I'd certainly argue that Macbeth, the eponymous protagonist of Shakespeare's play, is a powerful character. His rise from 'valiant' soldier to King of Scotland is a quick and violent one, and sees him shedding the blood of his best friend, the rightful king, and innocent women and children. His power is unquestionable in its tyranny – but not in its morality. I believe Shakespeare is showing us the discrepancy between two types of power – martial power, and the power of the moral conscience. It is the latter where Macbeth seems much weaker, and much more susceptible to the influence of external forces.

My conclusion might go something like this:

To conclude, Shakespeare shows us that Macbeth is an undeniably powerful character in the tyrannical, martial sense – but not in the moral sense. I find it fascinating how Shakespeare uses the character to show us the different aspects of power, and to show the audience which aspect is more valuable.

Good – something like this works well. It's easy to write, because I'm just reiterating my central argument from the intro. It helps with credit for AO2, by discussing the deeper ideas in the play about "power". It also helps with AO4 credit by commenting on a way I am personally struck by the text.

There's no need for it to be any longer – two sentences get the job done here.

But what about **a really strong conclusion**? The approach above can work fine, but if you are really going all-guns-blazing to impress the examiner, and you've got a the time available, you'll want to do something more ambitious.

A really strong conclusion will show some development in your argument. You've started your essay with an argument in your intro, your main paragraphs have justified that argument, and your (really strong) conclusion will show how your argument has become deeper, or more complex, or more interesting, due to what you have analysed in the main paragraphs.

This can be difficult! It needs you to look back over your essay and it needs you to think carefully – tough to do when the clock is ticking ever more loudly!

I've just looked back at my example paragraphs, and I notice that I've certainly analysed how Shakespeare shows different types of power (the martial, the moral, etc.) which is what I argued in the intro. But I also notice that "power" in Shakespeare's play often comes from sources that might be unexpected, especially considering the era in which the play was written and first performed. We see the power of the female triumphing over the power of the male; we see the power of compassion being more highly valued than the power of brutal force. I think that's quite interesting, and I'm going to use it as development in my conclusion here:

To conclude, I believe Shakespeare shows us a Macbeth who is powerful in a martial sense, but not powerful on more profound levels, such as moral strength. I find it interesting how true power in the play comes from sources such as the female (Lady Macbeth and the witches) and compassion (Malcolm), which is particularly surprising considering the era in which the play was written. I think Shakespeare was challenging the norms and expectations his audience would have been familiar with.

It's a bit longer, and takes more thought/time to write, but it shows insightful development of the central argument. Let's move on to a different section of the exam.

2) POETRY

For the next example, we'll work with the poetry section of the prose and poetry paper. This is the section where you are asked to write an answer for one of the poems you have studied in school. You can choose from two of the poems you have studied. The poems themselves are printed in the paper.

Writing a poetry essay uses the same kind of approach and structure as the other literature essays, so please do read through the previous section on the drama example if you haven't yet.

When answering the poetry question, we still use the same fundamental essay approaches as we use in the drama and prose questions. We give our central argument in the introduction, and justify that argument in our three main analytical paragraphs.

But there are some specific differences to consider when writing about poetry, so let's look over those first.

WHAT'S DIFFERENT ABOUT POETRY ESSAYS?

1) Coverage. When we write a whole-text answer for a play or novel, we're free to select the details from anywhere in the entire text that work for our argument. When writing on a poem, we've only got one short text and we need to cover as much of it as possible. This often means poetry essays have a higher density of quotations.

2) Musicality. Poems originated in a time when literature was listened to, rather than read off a page. This means we need to be attentive to how a poem sounds when we write an essay about it. We need to consider aspects such as rhyme, rhythm, auditory devices such as sibilance, alliteration, assonance, etc. We need to write about how the poet has used these devices to affect the sound, or musicality, of the poem, and the poet's reasons for doing so.

3) Structuring your answer. Because we're dealing with a much shorter text, it can be more difficult to find three different paragraph

topics for your three main paragraphs. We'll look at this more in the "planning and structuring" section of the example essay below.

COMMON PITFALLS

Even good candidates can succumb to these pitfalls when writing about poetry:

1) Focusing too much on details and not enough on the "big picture". Examiners often see essays where the candidate does really nice analysis of language details – particular devices or words – but doesn't engage with what the poem's actually about, or its deeper ideas (themes).

2) Not treating the poem as a poem. Many candidates don't give enough, or any, analysis of the poetic aspects of a poem. Writing about the poem's **form and structure** is what's needed.

3) Conflating the poet with the speaker. A lot of students in their poetry essays make an assumption that the poem is about the poet, especially with poems that are written in a first-person perspective. Always distinguish between the poet and **the speaker**, which is the term we use to refer to the narrator of the poem. Sometimes, poems are autobiographical (they are about the poet), but we should still explain in our introduction why we think the poem is autobiographical.

WHAT ARE FORM AND STRUCTURE?

'Form' refers to the shape and sound of a poem. How it looks on the page, and how it sounds, are things to think about. Form includes:

- o Rhyme. Is there a regular rhyme scheme in the poem? Irregular rhyme? Occasional occurrences of rhyme? Internal rhyme? A total lack of rhyme? What effect does this bring to the poem?
- o Rhythm. As above – we look for the regularity or irregularity of the rhythm, and consider why the poet uses such a rhythm.

o "Type" of poem. Some poems have a specific, named form –
e.g. a sonnet, a villanelle, or a haiku. It can sometimes be
useful to analyse the poet's choice of form in these cases. For
example, Wilfred Owen's poem "Anthem for Doomed Youth"
is about soldiers dying in war, but it's written in the form of
a sonnet. Sonnets traditionally deal with love and romance,
so it would be good to discuss in an essay why you think
Owen uses this form for a poem on such a brutal theme.

'Structure' refers to how the poem is organised – more specifically,
how the ideas in the poem are organised. Let's look at a short poem
called "Fish" to see an example:

Fish

*Sometimes silver flashes, sometimes kaleidoscopic
rainbows. They are treasures beneath the waves.*

*But sink too far and you'll find their teeth
are sharp; their blank eyes unforgiving.*

What's special about the structure – how the ideas are organised?
Well, the first stanza seems to focus on positive/benevolent aspects
of the fish such as their bright colours. The second stanza focuses
on the more negative, menacing aspects of the fish.

Therefore this poem features a common structural device called a
volta, which comes between the first and second stanza. A volta is
the point where there's a clear change in the poem's focus, or the
tone, or the ideas.

If we were to analyse the structure of "Fish", we might discuss why
the poet begins with the positive and ends with the negative. Why
do it this way rather than end with the positive? What effect does
this particular structure have?

"Fish" also has some enjambment, a structural device where a
sentence continues beyond the end of a line and there's no

punctuation at the end of the line. See lines 1 and 3. Lines 2 and 4 are "end stopped" – they finish with a full stop. Enjambment often causes particular words/phrases/ideas to be highlighted to the reader. "Rainbows", "teeth", the "sharpness" of the teeth are all things highlighted by the enjambment here.

Beginnings and endings of poems are useful to look at for ideas about structure. Does the poem you're writing about finish in a similar way to how it begins, or is there something very different? You can also look at smaller-scale structures such as sentence structure and word order (syntax).

There's quite a bit of overlap between form and structure, and sometimes it's hard to know which you're writing about. For example, it can often be good to write about the poem's stanzas – whether it has one long stanza, or several stanzas all of the same size, or stanzas or different sizes. This is both form and structure, because it's something that affects the shape of the poem but also how it's organised. It doesn't matter – so long as you're analysing the stanzas, you don't need to identify it as a particular aspect of "form" or "structure".

AN EXAMPLE POETRY ANSWER

In this section, I'm going to use Elizabeth Barrett Browning's poem "How do I love thee?". This might be one of the poems you've studied, but it doesn't matter if not. Concentrate on the approach and techniques we discuss, and apply them to your own poems when writing practice answers on them.

If you're reading the digital version of this book, you might want to get a copy of the poem on a different screen or print it out, as I'm going to be referring to it quite a bit. Here is the poem:

HOW DO I LOVE THEE? Elizabeth Barrett Browning

How do I love thee? Let me count the ways.
I love thee to the depth and breadth and height
My soul can reach, when feeling out of sight
For the ends of being and ideal grace.
I love thee to the level of every day's
Most quiet need, by sun and candle-light.
I love thee freely, as men strive for right.
I love thee purely, as they turn from praise.
I love thee with the passion put to use
In my old griefs, and with my childhood's faith.
I love thee with a love I seemed to lose
With my lost saints. I love thee with the breath,
Smiles, tears, of all my life; and, if God choose,
I shall but love thee better after death.

EXAM QUESTION: How does Browning portray interesting ideas about love in this poem?

This is a very typical poetry question, which identifies a key theme of the poem (love) and asks you to respond to it. Poetry questions often fix on a theme in this way, or they can be more general questions such as "How does the poet make this such a moving/sad/powerful etc. poem?"

PLANNING AND STRUCTURING

Because you will have studied in class the poem you'll be writing about, you should be able to draw on your ideas about the poem to start forming a main argument. Let's have a quick look at this poem's ideas so we can talk about how to structure an answer.

I really like Browning's poem because it feels so personal and intimate. It talks about love in very figurative ways, but still feels really sincere in what it's saying. The speaker addresses a lover and talks about the "ways" she loves him. We might assume the speaker is based on Browning herself – she fell in love with Robert Browning, another poet, and there's references to things in her real life ("lost saints" probably refers to Browning's siblings, some of whom died young).

The poem gives a range of ideas about love. At the start, the speaker refers to love in quite physical ways, using physical dimensions (line 2) to convey the great feeling of love she has.

There's an interesting mix of ideas about love, on one hand, being fiercely passionate (lines 3 and 4) yet on the other hand being very quiet and calming (line 6).

There's a volta in the poem – did you notice? It comes at the end of the first eight lines (an octave) and marks the start of the last six lines (a sestet). This is the conventional place for a volta to appear in a Petrarchan sonnet, which is the form of this poem. Look back at it – how do you think the poem changes after the volta?

I think the sestet focuses more on how love has strengthened the speaker. We can call this the edifying property of love. "Edifying" means "building" – so it's as if love has built up or developed/improved the speaker. The very end of the poem even seems to suggest that love can allow the speaker to overcome death – she will continue loving even beyond the grave.

So whilst the octave focuses on portraying the different types and powers of love the speaker feels for her lover, the sestet focuses more on love's edifying nature.

Now I've got ideas on what the poem's saying about love, how do I structure these in an essay?

I could focus each one of my main paragraphs on a different type of love, or idea about love, so the structure of my essay might look like this:

- Intro
- Para 1: physical strength of love
- Para 2: love as passionate but also gentle
- Para 3: edifying nature of love
- Conclusion

Focusing on different thematic topics like this can work, and it's certainly how I'd structure a whole-text essay, but it can also be problematic in poetry essays.

I won't have many quotations to use for some topics, especially the first two, whereas I'll have plenty for the third topic – so there's a tricky imbalance. Also, it could be difficult to incorporate poetic aspects such as form into this structure. Form, structure etc. are relevant to all these topics so I'll probably end up repeating myself.

Instead, here's a different approach to the structure of the essay, and **this is the structure I generally recommend for poetry responses**:

- Intro
- Para 1: the thematic paragraph – here I focus on what the poem is saying about love, discussing the theme in depth across the whole poem.
- Para 2: form (how it affects ideas about love).
- Para 3: structure, perspective, and anything else about the poem's composition – analysing how the poet has used them to convey ideas about love.
- Conclusion

This sort of structure still leads to a nicely controlled essay, but has some comforting flexibility about it. The first main paragraph, where you're analysing the theme, and commenting on lots of language, can become quite long – I don't think long paragraphs are a problem, because they suggest well-developed argument, but you can always split them into shorter paragraphs at appropriate points. The second and third paragraphs can focus less on theme and more on whatever technical aspects of the poem you'd like to write about.

It can be tricky to keep the second and third main paragraphs relevant to the task and to your argument, but I'll show you how to do this in my example.

THE INTRODUCTION

As always, we need to make clear our central argument in response to the exam task. But introductions for poetry essays need to do something extra:

It's really important to start your introduction with an **overview** of the poem you're writing about.

An overview is very simply an explanation of what the poem is about. It's vitally important, because it shows the examiner that you have read and understood the poem. It also helps to show your 'big-picture' appreciation of the poem. As well as analysing the details, you also have a good sense of what the entire poem is about.

Aim for these three elements in your poetry introduction:

- o 1) an overview of the poem
- o 2) your central argument in response to the task
- o 3) some AO2 engagement – explain what you think the poem is saying about "love", or whatever the question is asking about.

Here's my example introduction for my essay on "How do I love thee?". A reminder of the exam question:

How does Browning portray interesting ideas about love in this poem?

Browning's poem features a speaker who seems to be addressing a lover. The poem focuses on the speaker's description of the love she feels and explores the complexities of love as a concept. It's possible the speaker is based on Browning herself, as she had a passionate romance and marriage with Robert Browning, another Victorian-era poet.

That's where my overview ends – now on to the central argument:

I find it really fascinating how the poem treats love in complex ways that you wouldn't necessarily expect in a conventional, stereotypical romantic poem. Browning explores how love can be both passionate and gentle, and how it can edify the person who experiences it. I feel Browning intends to show how "love" is something more than just an emotion; instead, it is a powerful force that can change people.

My central argument engages with AO2, the deeper ideas about "love", so I've got all three elements in this decently concise intro. The examiner gets a good sense of my personal interpretation and response to the poem, and I'm showing I've read the poem and have understood it as a whole, rather than just responding to isolated language details.

MAIN PARAGRAPHS

TEST! This time, I'm going to make a purposeful mistake somewhere in my main paragraph examples. See if you can spot it. Answer at the end of the section!

As per my plan, I start with the thematic paragraph, giving full discussion of what interesting ideas the poem is saying about love. I need to keep those ideas relevant to the ones I introduced in my central argument.

The approach is similar for other essays in other sections of the exams, as it's the same AOs we need to address (and the same mark scheme used for assessment).

Therefore, as in other essays, we start the main paragraph with a conceptual topic intro, move on to the analysis of details, and then finish the paragraph with a mini conclusion.

Keep your eye out for how I target each of the four AOs.

The idea that love is more than a mere emotion becomes apparent at the start of the poem, where the speaker claims to love the addressee to a "depth and breadth and height". Browning uses this tricolon of physical diction to give the sense that love has actual physical dimension. It gives me the impression that love has a tangible presence and a weighty force, an unexpected and interesting idea about love, and it's emphasised by the simple monosyllabic and polysyndetic structure of the image. I really like the way this forcefulness of love is developed when the speaker compares her feeling of love to every day's most "quiet need". This is an oxymoron, where "quiet" conveys the tranquillity love brings while "need" suggests the urgency and strength of the feeling. Part of what makes the poem so interesting is the pace, and Browning quickly moves on to compare love with profound concepts such as justice ("men strive for right") and modesty ("they turn from praise"). I think this quick pace, enhanced by the anaphoric repetition of "I love thee", really conveys the interesting complexity and intensity of love. This complexity is developed with another tricolon toward the poem's end, where Browning attributes love to "breath, smiles, tears" – I really like the intensity created by the asyndetic structure here. "Smiles" and "tears" clearly connote the broad emotional spectrum of love, while "breath" conveys something about the sheer vitality of love – it is as vital an experience to life as the process of breathing. The poem's concluding idea is remarkably interesting – the speaker's declaration that she will "love thee better after death" suggests the ultimate power of love is something that can outlast the physical human body and exist beyond the death of that body. I think Browning is keen to show how the concept of love is far greater than its conventional portrayal as a strong emotion – it is something that has real force and power, perhaps second only to "God".

Okay! Quite a long paragraph, but not to the extent that it becomes a mess. I'm careful to keep things focused and relevant – notice there are lots of "interesting"s to maintain relevance to the task keyword.

There is quite a bit of analytical terminology – tricolon, polysyndeton etc. – in my language comments. I go over the meaning of these in the "terminology" section later in the book.

My first paragraph puts specific focus on the theme, and analysis focuses on language. My next paragraph, as per the plan, will focus on the poem's form, while still keeping analysis tied to the "interesting ideas about love" task. Here goes:

I think Browning's choice of form is interesting, and important for the poem's point of exploring unexpected ideas about love. Browning chooses the sonnet form, which ostensibly is conventional as sonnets traditionally focus on love. But it's interesting how Browning uses the Petrarchan sonnet form, which is older than the Shakespearean sonnet. I think she does this to create irony – she uses the most traditional sonnet form to explore love in untraditional ways. Browning follows quite strictly the conventional rhyme scheme of the form, which leads to some interesting pairings. "Height", "sight" and "light" emphasise the idea about love being a tangible force, whereas "faith" and "breath", an intriguing half rhyme, alludes to the other extreme – that love is something beyond the physical, but is profound and vital. The rhythm is mainly regular iambic pentameter, which helps the sense of love as reliable and permanent, but has some interesting irregularities. There are spondaic stresses in "breath, smiles, tears" and the repeated "love thee" that break the rhythm but draw attention to the forcefulness of love. Overall, I think Browning's choice and use of form is clever and ironically highlights how love is more interesting and complex than it is traditionally portrayed.

That gives a well-developed analysis of the poem's form. It addresses the musicality of the text, which is so important when writing about poetry. The start of the paragraph doesn't have any quotations, but this doesn't matter because it's still analytical (I'm analysing the poet's choice of form). However, it is best to avoid long sections that have no quotations.

I'm building argument (by focusing at the end on how Browning's portrayal of love defies conventional expectations).

Don't worry if you're not familiar with the terminology I use when commenting on the rhythm. The "analytical terminology" section later goes over it, but the analysis would still work without the specific terms. Just commenting on the regularity of the rhythm instead of mentioning the specific "iambic" rhythm, and how stressed syllables are put next to each other (instead of referring to "spondaic" stresses) would still be fine.

On to the final main paragraph. As per the plan, I'm going to put focus on structure and perspective.

However, at this stage I also need to be mindful of any important details from the poem I haven't yet commented on (for good coverage). There's quite a bit in the second half – the stuff about "lost saints" etc. – I haven't addressed, so I'm going to make effort to incorporate it in the next paragraph.

Browning's handling of the poem's structure is also important for how she portrays the interesting complexity of love. As is conventional for the Petrarchan sonnet form, the poem has a volta between the octave and the sestet. After the octave focuses on describing the experience of love ("free", "pure", "ideal grace") the sestet shifts focus onto the edifying nature of love. I think it's really interesting how Browning implies love can "put to use" the "passion" of "old grief", as if love can repair darker emotions. The sestet feels

65

particularly personal and intimate, with lots of syntax putting focus on the speaker's self and the relationship with the addressee ("I love thee with a love"). The reference to the speaker's "lost saints" could allude to the siblings Browning lost at a young age, adding to the fascinating personal intensity of the poem. It's interesting how Browning chooses to use a first-person speaker, as it really highlights how love impacts and changes the person who feels it – I think this is conveyed more powerfully than a third-person perspective would allow.

Oh no...I'm running a bit short on time, and I haven't finished this paragraph with a mini conclusion to hit AO2. But never mind. Often it's fine to leave that out at the end of the third main paragraph, so long as you've got some time left to write your conclusion (where you hit AO2).

This paragraph has a good frequency of quotations – note how useful parentheses () can be when integrating quotations.

AO4 is targeted well. Notice how I put focus on how the poem "feels" ("the sestet feels particularly personal...") and the ideas the poem gives me – all good signposting of my personal response to the text.

CONCLUSION

Remember what to do in the conclusion: reinforce our central argument, with some development if possible, and make sure to target AO2 (deeper ideas) and AO4 (personal response).

To conclude, what makes the ideas about love in the poem so interesting is that they go beyond the traditional portrayal of love as a romantic concept. Browning shows how love is more than just a feeling, but a force that is as vital to life as breathing. It is both comforting and fiercely passionate. I really like how Browning portrays love as something that can repair – it feeds on our "grief" to give us something that can even last after death.

Job done. But remember the test – did you spot the mistake?

In the second main paragraph I recycled a quotation I'd already used in the first main paragraph – "breath, smiles, tears". Ouch. We should always avoid using the same quotation more than once, but it can be really hard not to do this in poetry.</p<

When I first used the quotation I should have developed my analysis with the comments about spondaic stress that I used after the second mention; this would have avoided the repetition.

3) PROSE, EXTRACT

In the prose and poetry paper, you can choose to write an essay about an extract from the novel you've studied or you can choose the whole-text question. Depending on which drama paper you are taking, you can choose between the extract and whole-text question or you answer one of each (check with your teacher if unsure which you're doing!).

With the extract question you're given a short bit of the text – maybe a page or so – in the exam paper, and you're asked a question about that extract.

Quite a few students feel the extract option is easier than the whole-text one. But what are some of the difficulties we should be aware of?

- o It can be harder to structure a full essay answer in an extract question. You've got only a short bit from the text to work with, so it can be more difficult to select a range of good paragraph topics.
- o Extract answers take away the difficulty of having to recall quotations from memory, but they give you a narrower range of quotations to work with. What if the extract doesn't have many instances of good language for analysis?
- o In extract answers, it's easy to fall into the trap of not showing your knowledge and understanding of the text as a whole. Candidates often put too much focus on the details in the extract and neglect what the whole extract, and the whole text, is about.

These difficulties are good to be aware of when deciding whether to take the extract question. Check the given extract will give ideas for good topics and enough useful quotations for analysis.

EXTRACTS – A GENERAL PRINCIPLE

When writing extract essays, we should be focusing analysis on the extract itself. Don't start in-depth analysis of quotations from elsewhere in the text.

However, we should also be showing our understanding of the wider text. Therefore, making brief links to other parts of the text is good to do on occasion. When doing this, you can quote from other sections of the text if you can remember an appropriate quotation. Don't analyse the quotation.

Examiners watch for candidates who haven't studied the text very well, and who may not know much more about the text beyond what the exam paper gives them in the extract. So take opportunities to show your wider knowledge of the text.

To emphasise: the most common way good candidates lose marks in their extract answers is by putting all their focus on the details in the extract, without giving any 'big-picture' understanding of what the extract, and the wider text, is really about.

EXTRACT EXAMPLE

For this example, I'm going to use an extract from Charlotte Brontë's nineteenth-century novel "Jane Eyre". Remember, it doesn't matter if this isn't a text you've been studying (although I chose it because it comes up on the CIE syllabus), it's the approach, process and techniques we need to pay attention to.

"Jane Eyre" is a story about the protagonist, Jane, who has a pretty rough life. She's an orphan, and as a child is brought up by her aunt Miss Reed who treats her very badly. Then she's sent to boarding school, after which she finds work with the rich Mr Rochester and falls in love with him. Mr R. proposes marriage to her, but on their wedding day it's revealed he's already married – to a mad Jamaican woman he keeps locked in the attic of his house. Jane flees, unmarried, but (much) later returns, still in love with Mr R, and they do finally marry (the mad former wife died when she burned the house down, which also burned away Mr Rochester's eyesight...).

Autonomy is an important aspect of the novel's themes. For much of her life, Jane lacks autonomy (independence) – she is sent to places, she is proposed to rather than initiating proposals herself. The positive resolution comes when Jane chooses to go back to Mr R of her own autonomy. The tension between morality and pleasure is also important. Jane is often torn between doing the "right" thing and doing what she wants.

Here is the extract we'll use, from early in the story when young Jane is under the "care" of Miss Reed:

"What were you doing behind the curtain?" he asked.
"I was reading."
"Show the book."
I returned to the window and fetched it thence.
"You have no business to take our books; you are a dependent, mama says; you have no money; your father left you none; you ought to beg, and not to live here with gentlemen's children like us, and eat the same meals we do, and wear clothes at our mama's expense. Now, I'll teach you to rummage my bookshelves: for they are mine; all the house belongs to me, or will do in a few years. Go and stand by the door, out of the way of the mirror and the windows."
I did so, not at first aware what was his intention; but when I saw him lift and poise the book and stand in act to hurl it, I instinctively started aside with a cry of alarm: not soon enough, however; the volume was flung, it hit me, and I fell, striking my head against the door and cutting it. The cut bled, the pain was sharp: my terror had passed its climax; other feelings succeeded.
"Wicked and cruel boy!" I said. "You are like a murderer—you are like a slave-driver—you are like the Roman emperors!"

I had read Goldsmith's History of Rome, and had formed my opinion of Nero, Caligula, etc. Also I had drawn parallels in silence, which I never thought thus to have declared aloud.

"What! what!" he cried. "Did she say that to me? Did you hear her, Eliza and Georgiana? Won't I tell mama? but first—"

He ran headlong at me: I felt him grasp my hair and my shoulder: he had closed with a desperate thing. I really saw in him a tyrant, a murderer. I felt a drop or two of blood from my head trickle down my neck, and was sensible of somewhat pungent suffering: these sensations for the time predominated over fear, and I received him in frantic sort. I don't very well know what I did with my hands, but he called me "Rat! Rat!" and bellowed out aloud. Aid was near him: Eliza and Georgiana had run for Mrs. Reed, who was gone upstairs: she now came upon the scene, followed by Bessie and her maid Abbot. We were parted: I heard the words—

"Dear! dear! What a fury to fly at Master John!"

"Did ever anybody see such a picture of passion!"

Then Mrs. Reed subjoined—

"Take her away to the red-room, and lock her in there." Four hands were immediately laid upon me, and I was borne upstairs

QUESTION: How does Brontë's writing make you sympathise with Jane's character in this extract?

Think about how the examiners will use a question like this to differentiate the good answers from the average. Average responses will look quite superficially at what happens to Jane in the extract (she's abused, locked away) and use those as arguments for why we sympathise with her. Better answers will consider the novel's broader themes – the lack of autonomy, for example, seems to be important in this extract.

Always think about the whole novel's important themes when looking for topics to write about in your answer.

PLANNING AND STRUCTURING

Thinking caps on! Remember the planning stage is where a lot of the magic happens. We need not worry about trying to find the "right" ideas to use in our essay, we just need to think of interesting, justifiable ideas. Be confident and imaginative.

Quite often when I plan essays I think first of my central argument in response to the task, and then decide how I can break that argument into three main-paragraph topics. But on this occasion I'll do it the other way. I'll pick my paragraph topics and then see what central argument can link them together.

There are some glaringly obvious reasons why the reader will sympathise with Jane in this extract – the poor girl has books thrown at her and is subsequently dragged off to be locked in a room. We want to acknowledge those obvious reasons, perhaps in the intro, but our main paragraphs ideally should focus on more profound ideas.

We must exercise that crucial strategy of thinking about the whole text's main themes, and see if they are important in the extract.

As mentioned above, individual autonomy is important in "Jane Eyre" and in the extract. Jane has no autonomy (independence/free will); she is controlled by others. This lack of autonomy elicits sympathy from the reader.

Tensions around moral integrity is another important whole-text theme, and I can use that here too. Jane's morality elevates her in the reader's eyes above John and other characters, and causes us to sympathise with her.

Those topics should work really well, because they're tied to the whole text's themes so will help me to show I have strong, broad understanding of the text beyond the extract itself.

For my third topic, I'm going to do something similar to the poetry example, and veer more toward a technical focus than a thematic one. I'll focus on how the author orchestrates the relationship between the reader and the character, developing ideas from the previous paragraph. Commenting on narrative perspective (which should always be done in a prose essay) will fit well here.

This gives me a planned structure like this:

- o Main para 1: Jane's lack of autonomy
- o Main para 2: Jane's moral integrity (vs other chars)
- o Main para 3: author's shaping of the reader-character relationship

Hmm...now how to tie these together with a central argument? Well, looking at my plan, and thinking of the extract, it strikes me that what Jane experiences, although shocking, isn't entirely alien to me/us. She experiences a form of oppression that echoes things probably lots of us have been through or witnessed. It's the fact that Jane's suffering strikes a chord of familiarity with the reader that makes us feel such sympathy toward her.

INTRODUCTION

There are several specific things to do in an extract introduction that can help a great deal in scoring high marks. This means extract intros tend to be longer than others if they're done well.

Here's what to do to get a good extract intro:

1) Give an **overview** of the extract and **contextualise** the extract.

These should be done first in the intro – overview can come first, or context can come first.

An "overview" here is exactly the same as in the poetry essay. We need to give a clear explanation of **what happens in the extract**, showing our understanding of what the extract is about. So many candidates miss this, and it's really important to show the examiner that you have been able to read and understand the extract. It also helps a great deal in showing your "big-picture" appreciation of the extract.

"Contextualising the extract" means making it clear whereabouts in the text the extract comes from – what part of the whole story, what happens before and after, that sort of thing. It doesn't need to be done in great depth, but it helps show your knowledge of the wider text for AO1, and helps show that you know more of the text beyond what's given in the extract.

2) Establish your central argument – similar to what we do in other intros.

3) Engage with AO2 – explain the deeper ideas the writer is conveying in the extract. This is also similar to what we do in other intros.

The overview and the context are what make extract intros different, so let's use the plan above and look at an example of how to do it:

This extract comes toward the beginning of the novel, where the young orphan Jane Eyre is living under the guardianship of her aunt Miss Reed. Here, Jane suffers terribly at the hands of her cousin John, who abuses her emotionally (by undermining and ostracising her) and physically (by throwing a book at her head). Under instructions of her aunt, Jane is then taken to be locked in the "red room". This moment marks an important stage in the novel's narrative arc, as shortly after this Jane is sent away to Lowood School. But the extract also serves as a foreshadowing of the kind of relationships Jane will have with characters later in the story, particularly Mr Rochester. I think the main way Brontë makes me sympathise with Jane is by making the suffering she goes through quite familiar and relatable, albeit shocking. Jane's autonomy is stripped from her; she acts with integrity despite being treated with none. Brontë is not only foreshadowing what happens to Jane, but is also echoing the type of injustice we see and experience in our own world.

See what I mean by intros being quite long for the extract answer? We do need to be careful, and not let it get *too* long, as the examiner wants to see us getting into detailed analysis of the extract.

But the above example is good – both in terms of length and what it accomplishes:

There's a clear central argument which engages with the text's/writer's themes.

There's a clear overview of the extract, showing I've read and understood it well.

There's some quite thorough contextualisation, which shows my knowledge and understanding of the text beyond the extract.

Doing these things in the intro will really help to distinguish you from the (large number of) candidates who zoom straight into the extract's language details and don't consider the "big picture"

MAIN PARAGRAPHS

We take pretty much the same approach to main paragraphs as with other sections of the exam. Let's have a quick recap of what we're aiming for:

- o AO1: good use and handling of quotations; knowledge of the text; good writing
- o AO2: good understanding, engaging with the text's deeper ideas
- o AO3: insightful, developed analysis – keep focus on what the writer's doing
- o AO4: good sense of personal engagement with the text.

Extract essays are like poetry essays because, for the highest marks, there's pressure to cover the extract well. We need to be jamming in a good range of quotations, and not miss any important ones. Let's go:

The way Brontë portrays Jane as being stripped of all autonomy makes me feel really sympathetic toward her. Right from the outset, she is subjected to the oppressive interrogatives and imperatives of John, who demands with blunt monosyllabism to know "what were you doing?" and orders her to "show the book". Brontë shapes the crude abruptness of his speech to show how he simply assumes he has the right of control over Jane. I find it upsetting the way Jane tells us "I did so" after being ordered to move by John; the simplicity of the language might make her obedience sound meek, but I think it leads the reader to pity the impossibility of her situation rather than to condemn her of weakness.* There is a moment of triumph in the extract where Jane does act with autonomy, accusing John of being "wicked and cruel", and of being "like a murderer...like a slave driver", after he assaults her. The elegant tautology of "wicked" and "cruel", along with the richness of her similes, juxtaposes with John's crude form of speech and aligns the reader with her – but Brontë is only doing this to really heighten our sympathy when Jane is punished for her autonomy and she is "taken away" to be "locked" in the dreaded red room. Brontë's description of "four hands...laying upon [Jane]" creates great pathos, and the dehumanised "hands" of the oppressing force form a strong visualisation of how Jane is utterly without autonomy. I think this is a really important prolepsis of how Jane's autonomy is threatened by Mr Rochester. She can only ultimately find happiness with him when she goes to him of her own will.

Ideally I'd like to do more on AO2 – more discussion of what Brontë's telling us about the importance of autonomy – but my para's getting long so I'll save it for my conclusion.

I like the comment which I've marked with an asterisk* at the end. Language such as "I did so" is quite difficult to analyse in a developed way, because there's not much to comment on beyond the simplicity of the language. What I've done here is evaluate (judge) how the reader responds to the language. This sort of evaluation is a great way to develop comment on language.

On to the next paragraph – the topic in my plan is Jane's morality contrasted with other characters.

Remember to try for a smooth transition between paragraphs – look how I do it here.

It's not just the profoundly harmful attack on Jane's autonomy that causes me to feel sympathetic; it's also the way Brontë shows how unjustly Jane is treated. She is a good character. There's something deeply upsetting about the situation Brontë contrives: a young girl, Jane, sat quietly by herself, reading a book, suddenly assaulted by a repugnant boy. John is just a little boy, his only power over her is granted by material status that makes him a "gentleman's child" and her a "dependent" who must "beg". The writer portrays Jane as a stoic who quietly endures the abuse in a curiously unemotional way. Apart from brief mention of her "terror passing" and her "cry of alarm", Brontë makes no mention of Jane's emotions. She does not cry. Personally, I think this creates more sympathy in the reader than a character who reacts with emotional outbursts, and it makes John and his outbursts ("he called me 'rat! rat!' and bellowed aloud") seem more immature. Her emotional integrity also contrasts with his brash, aggressive physicality wherein he "runs headlong" at her and "grasps" at her. Brontë develops the integrity of Jane by characterising her intelligence: there's an elevated but not arrogant diction in Jane's speech and thoughts, with words such as "tyrant" and "petulant", which combines with the fact that she uses books to educate herself about "Roman emperors" instead of weaponising them like John. The character's stoicism and intelligence build an integrity that evokes reader sympathy, but also highlights the injustice of the abuse Jane receives.

My mini conclusion to this paragraph gives a clear final analysis of the writer's method and intention, but again leaves me room to develop AO2 comment in the final concluding paragraph.

The start of this paragraph is light on quotations, but it's still analytical – there's a clear focus on what the writer is doing. This only works because I phrase it carefully. I write about "the situation Brontë contrives" (contrives means "designs") to keep focus on the writer's method.

The final main paragraph, as per the plan, puts focus on narrative perspective and the way the writer shapes the reader-character relationship:

The strong pathos I feel for Jane is largely due to the way Brontë orchestrates the relationship between the protagonist and reader, and the narrative perspective is a key part of this relationship. Brontë uses Jane's homodiegetic perspective to make us feel closer to the character, as the story is related to us directly through the voice of the character. And it's the close, intimate way it's related that creates such strong sympathy. When Jane acknowledges the "drop or two of blood trickling down [her] neck" and the "sharp pain", it comes across as a private, personal admission of suffering rather than a mere description, and that's because of the perspective Brontë uses. Jane's first-person account reveals important details that a third-person couldn't, such as her "not knowing what she did with [her] hands" when John attacks her. Brontë implies that Jane fights back, but the narrator doesn't acknowledge this, because to do so would risk her seeming prideful. The writer is carefully shaping the reader's relationship with Jane, encouraging admiration of her humility rather than condemnation of her arrogance.

"Narrative perspective" is a feature quite particular to prose writing, where there's always a narrator (unlike in drama), so it's good to write about it in your prose essay. One way to approach it, as I've done here, is to analyse how the perspective influences readers' relationships with the character, or the reader's impressions of character. Brontë uses a first-person perspective – I refer to this as "homodiegetic" just for some fancy terminology to help AO1. See the later "terminology" section for a fuller explanation.

CONCLUSION

As always, we're looking to reinforce our central argument, hopefully with some development, and make sure we hit AO2 and AO4. My main-paragraph conclusions have been a bit light on AO2, so I'm going to make sure I address it fully here:

Overall, Brontë is taking great strides to situate Jane's character as a victim of oppression and to align sympathy with us. I think the way Brontë shows how unjustly Jane is treated creates a lot of sympathy, but it's the overwhelming attack on her autonomy that I find most powerful. It's important for the novel as a whole – Jane must find means to exercise autonomy in order to find happiness – but I think Brontë's showing us a lot about the real world, too. The brutal, violent denial of Jane's autonomy is a dramatisation of our own reality. In my opinion, that's what the novel is really about: discovering the power of your own autonomy.

Remember the ITTIRA sentence I spoke about in part one? I put it to use at the end of this conclusion.

4) UNSEEN

Depending on which components you're taking, you may have to tackle the "unseen" paper (paper 4).

If you're not sure whether you're doing this or not, don't panic. It's hard to keep track of these things when you've got so many different subjects to deal with. You may have been given an overview sheet in your English class which details all the exams you are taking, but in any case just check with your teacher – and keep checking as many times as you need!

In the unseen section, you write about a poem OR a prose extract (your choice) which you won't have seen before you open the paper.

Sounds bad, but on the bright side you get a bit longer (one hour and fifteen minutes) than the other exams. The exam board recommend you spend about twenty minutes of that time reading and planning.

It can seem daunting, but approach it with confidence – this paper is a really good opportunity for showing off your skills and for distinguishing yourself above other candidates.

The approach is very similar to other exams. You must meet the same four assessment objectives, and the mark scheme is the same. In terms of structuring your answer, and the techniques used in your answer, it's the same as other papers we've already been through.

One different thing is the question – it will still be an analytical ("how does the writer") sort of question, but the paper will give you a list of three bullet-pointed prompts which are designed to help you think about the text.

These three bullet-points can be a great help with the structure of your essay – they work well as paragraph topics.

THE BIG CHALLENGE

The first engagement with the unseen text is perhaps the most challenging moment: you've opened the paper, read the unseen text/s, and you're thinking: what on earth is this about?

Remember the examiners aren't looking for a "correct" interpretation. They're looking for *your* interpretation. They want to see that you've read the text and come up with your own ideas as to *what it's really about*.

One of the worst things to do in the unseen is to "dodge" the interpretation. A lot of candidates attempt to give an answer without ever engaging with what the text is about.

FIRST INTERPRETATION

Let's practise a simple but effective way of confronting that big challenge of interpreting the text. This uses an exercise called "identifying theme", because it's a good way of thinking of the text's deeper ideas (theme).

Here's the process:

1) read the text.

2) Write down this sentence and fill in the blank with one word (or short phrase – but it should be just one thing):

This text is about _____.

The word you put in the gap should ideally be an **abstract noun**. This means an idea, emotion, concept. These work better here than concrete nouns, which are physical things (dog, table, house).

3) Below your first sentence, answer the following question:

What is the text saying about _____ (the word you used to fill the gap).

Here, your answer should be a bit longer – a sentence, giving a full, clear idea of what the text is saying about the thing you identified.

Let's practise using this haiku by the Japanese poet Yosa Buson:

The light of a candle
Is transferred to another candle—
Spring twilight

Try steps 1) and 2) above.

Remember, don't worry about finding the "correct" idea. Believe in your own idea.

Here's what I wrote for 1): *This text is about light*. "Light" really is a concrete noun. Abstract nouns are often best to use, but sometimes concrete nouns are a better fit.

And my answer for 2): *The text is saying that light never dies; it's always passed on to something new.*

And just like that I've got an interpretation of the deeper message given by the text.

More practice: have a go with an excerpt from Charles Dickens' "David Copperfield, and then with William Ernest Henley's poem "Invictus". Do steps 1) and 2) for each text.

If I may so ex-press it, I was steeped in Dora. I was not merely over head and ears in love with her, but I was saturated through and through. Enough love might have been wrung out of me, metaphorically speaking, to drown anybody in; and yet there would have remained enough within me, and all over me, to pervade my entire existence.

Out of the night that covers me,
Black as the pit from pole to pole,
I thank whatever gods may be
For my unconquerable soul.

In the fell clutch of circumstance
I have not winced nor cried aloud.
Under the bludgeonings of chance
My head is bloody, but unbowed.

Beyond this place of wrath and tears
Looms but the Horror of the shade,
And yet the menace of the years
Finds and shall find me unafraid.

It matters not how strait the gate,
How charged with punishments the scroll,
I am the master of my fate,
I am the captain of my soul.

Here's what I wrote for the Dickens excerpt:

1) This text is about love. 2) The text is saying that love is completely overwhelming, to the point that it dominates someone's life.

And for the poem:

1) This text is about free will. 2) The text is saying that we can overcome any difficulty so long as we remain in charge of our own free will.

It doesn't matter if your answer is different to mine – hopefully it is different! But you've drawn an interpretation from what you've read, so you can justify it by referring to details in the text. And you've done something many candidates won't do: shape an understanding of what the text is really about!

EXAMPLE ANSWER

We'll use a prose extract for our example. Remember, in the exam you can choose the poem OR the prose extract. Personally, I think the prose extract tends to be more difficult when it comes to shaping good, interesting interpretations, which is why I'm using the prose here. Poems tend to be easier to interpret. Don't let that put you off taking the prose option. If fewer candidates opt for the prose, your answer will have a better chance of standing out to the examiner.

The exam papers don't tend to identify the name of the story/novel, but they do give a bit of context to explain what's going on. So here's what the exam paper would look like:

EXAM QUESTION:

Read carefully the following extract from a novel. In this extract, the narrator (Lockwood) is staying overnight at the house owned by Heathcliff, and receives an unexpected visitor called Catherine Linton.

How does the writer make this moment so memorable for you?

To help you answer this question, you might consider:

- How the writer shapes the atmosphere.
- How the writer portrays Lockwood's reaction to Catherine.
- How the writer portrays Catherine's character.

The question itself is quite broad, but the list gives us useful topics to focus analysis on in each main paragraph.

Let's read the extract – but do read it carefully. Often extracts contain a kind of trick to weed out candidates who read carefully, and those who don't. Here, you should pay special attention to Catherine – think about who she really might be.

Be warned – there's some quite nasty stuff in this extract (some violent imagery of skin being cut on broken glass along with subsequent bleeding).

I heard distinctly the gusty wind, and the driving of the snow; I heard, also, the fir bough repeat its teasing sound, and ascribed it to the right cause: but it annoyed me so much, that I resolved to silence it, if possible; and, I thought, I rose and endeavoured

84

to unhasp the casement. The hook was soldered into the staple: a circumstance observed by me when awake, but forgotten. "I must stop it, nevertheless!" I muttered, knocking my knuckles through the glass, and stretching an arm out to seize the importunate branch; instead of which, my fingers closed on the fingers of a little, ice-cold hand!

The intense horror of nightmare came over me: I tried to draw back my arm, but the hand clung to it, and a most melancholy voice sobbed,

"Let me in—let me in!"

"Who are you?" I asked, struggling, meanwhile, to disengage myself.

"Catherine Linton," it replied, shiveringly (why did I think of Linton? I had read Earnshaw twenty times for Linton)—"I'm come home: I'd lost my way on the moor!"

As it spoke, I discerned, obscurely, a child's face looking through the window. Terror made me cruel; and, finding it useless to attempt shaking the creature off, I pulled its wrist on to the broken pane, and rubbed it to and fro till the blood ran down and soaked the bedclothes: still it wailed, "Let me in!" and maintained its tenacious grip, almost maddening me with fear.

"How can I!" I said at length. "Let me go, if you want me to let you in!"

The fingers relaxed, I snatched mine through the hole, hurriedly piled the books up in a pyramid against it, and stopped my ears to exclude the lamentable prayer.

I seemed to keep them closed above a quarter of an hour; yet, the instant I listened again, there was the doleful cry moaning on!

"Begone!" I shouted. "I'll never let you in, not if you beg for twenty years."

"It is twenty years," mourned the voice: "twenty years. I've been a waif for twenty years!"

Thereat began a feeble scratching outside, and the pile of books moved as if thrust forward.

85

I tried to jump up; but could not stir a limb; and so yelled aloud, in a frenzy of fright.

To my confusion, I discovered the yell was not ideal: hasty footsteps approached my chamber door; somebody pushed it open, with a vigorous hand, and a light glimmered through the squares at the top of the bed. I sat shuddering, yet, and wiping the perspiration from my forehead: the intruder appeared to hesitate, and muttered to himself.

At last, he said, in a half-whisper, plainly not expecting an answer,

"Is any one here?"

I considered it best to confess my presence; for I knew Heathcliff's accents, and feared he might search further, if I kept quiet.

With this intention, I turned and opened the panels. I shall not soon forget the effect my action produced.

Heathcliff stood near the entrance, in his shirt and trousers; with a candle dripping over his fingers, and his face as white as the wall behind him. The first creak of the oak startled him like an electric shock: the light leaped from his hold to a distance of some feet, and his agitation was so extreme, that he could hardly pick it up.

"It is only your guest, sir," I called out, desirous to spare him the humiliation of exposing his cowardice further. "I had the misfortune to scream in my sleep, owing to a frightful nightmare. I'm sorry I disturbed you."

(waif = homeless child)

The examiners will want to see in your answer a full understanding of the text. They want to see that you've read it carefully and picked up on details that shape your interpretation.

Did you spot anything unusual about Catherine? Spoiler alert: she's not really a person, she's a ghost! Well done if you worked it out.

There are some clues such as her moaning noise, and how she's been a "waif" for so many years. It's quite difficult, but it's an example of the sort of "trick" the exam board can throw in, and shows how it's worth reading very carefully.

There are other key details that might affect our understanding of the extract:

Right at the end, Lockwood says to Heathcliff that he'd been having a "frightful nightmare". It's an easy detail to miss, but it throws up the possibility that the whole encounter with Catherine didn't actually happen. Does the writing suggest to you that it was real, or just a dream? Discussing your thoughts in your answer would help develop your interpretation and personal response.

Why does Lockwood feel he must "confess his presence" to Heathcliff? Does this language suggest Lockwood has been somewhere in the house where he shouldn't have been?

Furthermore, what's odd about Heathcliff at the end? According to the paper, Heathcliff is the owner of the house where Lockwood is staying. At the end of the extract, Heathcliff seems to be really freaked out by something – he looks as if "startled by an electric shock" etc. Lockwood thinks Heathcliff's just surprised to see him, but is there a hidden implication here? Is it possible that Heathcliff heard the ghost, and knows something about it?

When you read the unseen text, have a really sharp eye open for details like these and think about how they affect your interpretation.

So what's the extract about? A random guy being visited by a ghost? Really, we want a deeper interpretation, so try running the "identifying theme" exercise, completing steps 1) and 2) for the extract.

It will be more difficult this time. Often it is with prose extracts, where themes aren't so apparent as in poetry. Take some time to give it some thought.

There are many possibilities, and your ideas will be different to mine. For 1), things like "fear", "horror", "loneliness" might fit well, but it's perfectly fine if you saw something else.

I need something to use for the rest of the example, so I'm going to go with "the unknown" as my response to 1). I feel like this extract is all about the unknown – Lockwood is subjected to an unknown being whose weirdly floating outside his bedroom window (presumably upstairs), but there's also an unknown past that the ghost/Catherine belongs to.

For 2), I think the text is saying how horrifying and confusing it can be when we're confronted with the unknown. It causes us to do things we'd never normally do (e.g. I hope Lockwood doesn't make a habit of violently assaulting young girls).

Getting some thoughts on the text's deeper ideas in that way can really help the strength of your answer.

EXAMINER LIKES AND DISLIKES

Here are some of the things examiners like to see in unseen answers and some things they don't like.

Likes:

Evidence of planning. The examiner wants to see that you have thought about the text's deeper meaning before you start writing your answer. Often candidates will just start writing, and maybe toward the end of their answer start commenting on the deeper meaning of the text. Best to be doing this from the start.

Good introductions. It seems to be a thing with the unseen that candidates sometimes don't write any sort of introduction – they just go straight into addressing the bullet points. Writing a good intro can set your answer apart from the rest.

Sensitive responses to language – they want to see you analysing the language, picking up on key words and images.

All the usual AO stuff – nice handling of a good range of quotations (AO1), analytical treatment of narrative perspective (in prose) and form/structure (in verse) – AO3, thoughtful engagement with the text's deeper meaning (AO2) and clear personal engagement with the text and its ideas (AO4).

Dislikes:

Imbalanced coverage. They don't like it, for example, when candidates write lots about the start of an extract/poem but don't really deal with the ending. Make sure you're selecting details from the start, middle and end.

PLANNING

We've already got some of the planning done:

No need to mess about thinking of paragraph topics; we can just use the bullet points in the question.

We've done the "identifying theme" exercise to help form our argument.

We've picked out some key details that affect our interpretation.

What we should still do:

Highlight some key details in the extract – ones which are important for interpretation, and ones which are important for language, making sure we're covering the start, middle and end.

Jot down some questions to help shape our personal response. For example, with this extract:

Do I sympathise with Lockwood in this extract? Or do I condemn how he hurts Catherine?

How would the extract feel different if it were written in a third-person perspective instead of the first person?

What's the single most [memorable] part of the extract? (Adjust according to the question keyword).

And so on. You don't have to write down answers to these; as you work, you'll probably come to think of ideas you can include in your essay.

INTRODUCTION

Seeing as candidates often neglect the intro, it's worth doing it really well in order to distinguish your answer. The intro for the unseen is a bit different to other exams.

Overview: when writing about an unseen poem, always include in your intro an overview of what the poem's about, what's happening in it, to show your surface understanding. With the extract, be mindful not to simply repeat the overview already given in the question.

We do want to give a full overview of how we interpret and understand the extract. This can lead into AO2 comment on what the text is saying about the theme we've identified in it.

This question asks about how the writer has made this such a memorable moment. Let's go:

On the surface, this extract is certainly a memorable moment due to the very unusual encounter the writer presents between Lockwood and Catherine. The writer gives me the impression that the young girl outside Lockwood's window is in fact a ghost, what with her "doleful moaning" and insistence she's been a "waif for twenty years". But there's much ambiguity, which only makes it more memorable – the writer suggests at the end that it was nothing more than a "nightmare". Furthermore, the way Heathcliff's character seems so strongly "startled", as if struck by an "electric shock", implies that he may have heard the ghost himself. I feel this extract is about more than a possible ghostly encounter. It's exploring what it's like to be confronted with the unknown. Lockwood is in an unfamiliar, unknown place as a "guest", and is confronted by an unknown entity with an unknown history. The writer shows how the unknown can fling us into turmoil and make us behave in ways unknown to ourselves – as seen with what Lockwood does to Catherine's wrists..

This introduction engages with both the surface and deeper meanings of the text. It uses a lot of quotations, because I'm supporting my interpretation with examples from the text. Note that there's no analysis of the language in these quotations – we save that for main paragraphs. The intro also gives good conceptual engagement with the deeper ideas and intentions presented by the writer. Good stuff!

MAIN PARAGRAPHS

The first bullet point gives us the first topic: how the writer shapes the atmosphere. This is quite broad – it gives us a lot of room to analyse the mood, tone, and feeling of the place and encounter.

It needs a bit of careful management. All sections of the extract give opportunity for comment on the atmosphere, but I want to avoid overlap with the other bullet points/topics. So I won't do too much on the encounter itself in this paragraph, because the other topics will force me to focus on that. Instead, I'll mainly focus on the opening and ending to ensure good overall coverage of the extract. Do think about how you manage coverage across your topics.

The oppressive pathetic fallacy at the start of the extract immediately helps make the atmosphere memorable. The writer puts heavy emphasis on the forcefulness of the weather outside Lockwood's room with diction such as "gusty" and "driving". Lockwood's repetition of "I heard" when describing the noise of the wind and snow creates unease; it feels as if he is on high alert, for some reason having a heightened awareness. The personification of the fir branch "teasing" against the window makes the atmosphere outside feel more alien and unknown. Lockwood's turmoil when confronted with the unknown is highlighted by his remarkably drastic action of "knocking [his] knuckles through the glass" in order to silence the branch. When he realises he's holding someone's hand instead of the branch, I think the writer is turning a familiar situation (touching another person) into something really alarming and uncomfortable, which the sharp description of the "ice-cold" hand achieves. This builds a memorably uneasy, alien atmosphere which persists throughout the encounter and remains afterwards, when Heathcliff finds Lockwood. I think here the writer draws our attention to the possibility that there's something amiss with Heathcliff's reaction – he doesn't notice the hot candle wax "dripping over his fingers", and his face is as "white as the wall". It makes me feel that Heathcliff knows something about Catherine, but because the story is related to us through the first-person narration of Lockwood, it remains unknown to the reader. The writer gives me a really strong sense of how disorientating it is to be confronted with the unknown.

This paragraph puts consistent focus on the writer's methods and gives sensitive responses to a range of language details. It remains focused on the bullet point, whilst also building on the introduction's argument about the "unknown". It shows that the candidate is thinking about the meaning of the extract, and building his/her interpretation of it.

The next paragraph, according to the bullet points, should focus on Lockwood's reaction to Catherine (and how it makes the moment memorable).

Initially, the writer's use of ambiguity makes Lockwood's reaction to Catherine memorable. Although the encounter is not framed as if it is taking place in the narrator's sleep, when the girl grasps Lockwood's hand it is the "intense horror of nightmare" that he feels. Is it real or not? The writer keeps us confounded by the unknown. The writer builds on Lockwood's reaction of horror, describing how

*he "tried to draw back [his] arm but the hand clung to it",
straightforward diction giving a clear and unsettling implication of
the girl's supernatural strength. When the girl speaks her name, the
narrator questions "why did I think of Linton?" as if he himself
decided the name in a dream, which makes me feel even more
disorientated. The writer describes how "terror made [Lockwood] feel
cruel" when he sees Catherine's face, which seems to me an
incongruous reaction to seeing a little girl, but the aggression of the
word "cruel" shows how strong an impact this unknown situation has
on Lockwood. It's an impact the writer makes extremely shocking
and memorable when Lockwood proceeds to "pull its wrist on the
broken pane, and rub it to and fro, until blood dripped down".
Suddenly there's no ambiguity – the language is very clear,
heightening the shock felt by the reader at Lockwood's reaction. The
dehumanising use of "its" instead of "her" again shows how
Lockwood is transformed by the unknown into something
uncompassionate. When Lockwood declares "I'll never let you in, not
if you beg for twenty years", I think the writer uses the cruelty of his
tone to show how fear can transform a person. Overall, Lockwood's
reaction is a memorable demonstration by the writer of how fear of
the unknown so severely impacts us.*

A good range of language details, and careful management – the
focus is kept on Lockwood's reaction, but still builds argument about
the impact of the unknown. The writer's method is kept at the
forefront, and the paragraph concludes with discussion of the
writer's intention.

The third and final bullet point invites us to consider how Catherine
herself is portrayed. At this point, we need to be careful with the
details we select as we can't recycle quotations already used in the
first two main paragraphs.

*The way Catherine's portrayed by the writer is a big part of what
makes this extract so memorable for me, and the narrative
perspective plays an important role in this. Although the reader*

would naturally align with the first-person narrator, who's inevitably the closest character to the reader, I find myself distanced from Lockwood due to his response to the girl and I sympathise more with Catherine. Her "doleful moaning", which continues incessantly in the form of a "lamentable prayer" even after Lockwood has waited fifteen minutes for it to silence, makes heavy use of emotive diction that is both pitiable and ominous. Her simplistic, repetitive phrases of "let me in!" and "twenty years!" make her seem familiarly childlike yet we can't escape the implication of her supernatural presence. The writer is making her seem simultaneously familiar and unsettlingly unknown. The writer further highlights her familiar childishness with the slightly ungrammatical speech of "I'm come home; I'd lost my way" – but how can she have been lost for twenty years? She is disarmingly pitiable but is also an assault on our rationality. When Lockwood must listen to her "feeble scratching" outside his window, I'm torn between feeling sympathy for Lockwood and pity for her weakness conveyed by "feeble". The writer's structuring is impactful – Catherine is a dominating presence throughout the extract until suddenly she's gone: Heathcliff's "hasty footsteps" arrive and there's no more mention of the girl. It makes me think there's some sort of unknown relationship between Heathcliff and her, as if they can't exist in the same space.

This gives developed comment on the function of perspective, and much discussion of the conflicted response the reader feels toward Catherine. The ending is a bit light on AO2, but that's okay because the conclusion is next.

CONCLUSION

Here we bring everything together – we tie our opening central argument with the additional ideas we've discussed in the main paragraphs. We need to show the examiner our full, insightful understanding of the extract:

In conclusion, this extract provides on the surface a very memorable encounter between a man and a ghostly entity. But it's the writer's deeper ideas about being confronted with the unknown that I personally find truly memorable. The writer shows how the fear of something unknown has such terrible influence on Lockwood. Further than this, the reader is given a direct sense of being in conflict with the unknown: we're not sure whether to sympathise with Lockwood or be appalled by him; we're not sure whether Catherine is a pitiable young "waif" or a terrifying, inhuman "creature". We're not even sure whether the encounter happens in reality. Furthermore, it seems to me that all three characters are somewhat lonely. They are separated by different realms of existence or different layers of knowledge. The writer gives me such a strong sense of the isolating and disorientating impact of the unknown on us.

This ties the essay's ideas together well and gives development of the opening argument. It targets AO2 by considering the writer's intentions regarding theme, and it reflects on the reader's response to the extract. Job done.

PART 3: APPENDIX

ANALYTICAL TERMINOLOGY

In this section, we'll look at some examples of terminology that might help in your analyses. We'll focus on more unusual terms rather than those you're probably already familiar with (such as simile, metaphor, alliteration, etc.)

For writing about drama

Stichomythia

This occurs quite frequently in drama. Stichomythia is when two characters speak together, each character only saying one line before swapping to the other character, who also says one line. It looks like this example from "Romeo and Juliet":

> PARIS: *Happily met, my lady and my wife.*
> JULIET: *That may be, sir, when I may be a wife.*
> PARIS: *That may be must be, love, on Thursday next.*
> JULIET: *What must be, shall be.*

Often, as in this example, it shapes quite a tense dynamic between characters (Juliet does not want to marry Paris, but he's really keen). Other times it can shape a more harmonious dynamic.

You can comment on how the playwright uses stichomythia, or how a section of the dialogue has stichomythic form.

Apostrophe

(Not the punctuation mark.) In drama texts, apostrophe is a type of speech where the character talks directly to an object, or to some sort of abstract concept, or to a character who's not present on stage.

Shakespeare uses it a lot, for example when Macbeth speaks directly to the dagger in act two. It can also occur in poetry, for example in John Donne's "Death be not Proud":

Death, be not proud, though some have called thee
Mighty and dreadful, for thou are not so.

Paralinguistics

This refers to any type of language beyond the spoken/written word. It's a useful term for referring to a character's movements, facial expression, etc. You can comment on how the playwright shapes the character's paralinguistic features for specific effects.

Monologue and soliloquy

Both are forms of dialogue where one character gives a speech. A monologue is a speech directed to a listener(s), which could be another character or the audience. A soliloquy is a speech which is not directed to any recipient – often used to give voice to a character's internal thoughts.

Alignment

Very useful for drama or any text featuring characters. Alignment refers to the audience's/reader's feelings toward a character. Does the writer do something to make the audience like, or sympathise with, or be on the side of a character? Then the writer is aligning the audience with the character. You can also write about how the writer aligns the audience against other characters such as antagonists.

For writing about narrative perspective

Very useful when analysing prose, and sometimes in poetry.

A homodiegetic narrative perspective is when the narrator is also a character involved in the story. Often, first-person narrators are homodiegetic.

Heterodiegetic narrative perspectives involve a narrator or narrative voice that does not take part in the story. For example, some sections of "Wuthering Heights" use heterodiegetic narration. The character of Lockwood narrates the story of Heathcliff and Catherine's past, but only as it is told to him by another character. He is not involved in the story he is telling us. It can be useful to identify homo/heterodiegetic perspectives and to analyse how the writer uses them to shape reader relationships with characters and plot.

Retrospective narrative perspective involves a narrator looking back on the past and telling a story that occurred in the past. Common exam texts such as "Spies" and "A Separate Peace" feature retrospective perspectives; they often shape tension between the plot and the reader because retrospective perspectives have a degree of unreliability (false, weakened memories; reshaping the past, etc.).

Poetry terminology: rhyme

When writing about poetry, you may want to comment on rhyme scheme and terminology can help (but isn't obligatory).

Rhyme schemes are denoted using letters: an ABCB rhyme scheme is when the second and third lines end with the same rhyme. The first and final lines (in the four line stanza) don't rhyme.

Some common rhyme schemes have specific names:

Alternate rhyme

ABABAB... or ABABCDCDEFEF... (these can occur over just a couple of lines or over a whole poem).

Enclosed rhyme

 ABBA (the first and final lines share a rhyme; the second and third lines share a different rhyme).

Couplets

AABBCCDD...

Internal rhyme

When words within the same line, or in adjacent lines, rhyme. E.g.:

Our chin dangles toward our shoulder as we get older and wiser.

Half rhyme (or slant rhyme)

When words almost rhyme, but not quite. E.g. "book" and "shook"; "poor" and "soul".

Visual rhyme

When words look on the page as if they rhyme, but don't sound a rhyme. E.g. "fear" and "wear".

Poetry terminology: rhythm

You might also want to use specific terminology for different rhythms. This can be extremely difficult – I'd only recommend studying these terms if you've got a good ear for rhythm, and you can easily detect the stressed and unstressed syllables in a written text. Some people can; some can't.

The symbols u and / are used to denote rhythm. u = an unstressed syllable. / = a stressed syllable.

So the word "happy" would be denoted as: / u

(Two syllables; the first is stressed, the second unstressed.

The word "celebration" would be denoted as: / u / u

Iambic rhythm

u / u / u / ...

E.g.: "but soft! What light though yonder window breaks?"

Trochaic rhythm

/ u / u / u ... (the opposite of iambic)

E.g.: "Peter Piper picked a pepper".

Anapaestic rhythm

u u / u u / u u / ...

E.g.: "And no voice but was praising this Roland of mine,
As I poured down his throat our last measure of wine."

Dactylic rhythm

/ u u / u u / u u ... (the opposite of anapaestic)

E.g.: "Half a league, half a league,
Half a league onward,
All in the valley of Death."

(Notice the dactylic rhythm isn't strictly regular; it alters at the ends of these lines. But the verse features strong dactylic rhythm in the line openings.)

Spondaic rhythm

/ /

You'll never get a whole line of spondaic rhythm – it's impossible, because it means all syllables are stressed. But you do get lots of "spondaic stresses" in poetry, where adjacent syllables are stressed.

E.g.: "She turned to me with perfect grace and said, "Shut up!".

The line begins with regular iambic rhythm which is broken by the spondaic stress of "shut up". Spondaic stress is often used for emphasis, or to bring disruption to an otherwise harmonic tone. This can be really useful to look out for and comment on.

Poetry terminology: stanza sizes

A stanza with one line: monostich

A stanza with two lines: couplet

Three lines: tercet

Four lines: quatrain

Five lines: cinquain

Six lines: sestet

Seven lines: septet

Eight lines: octave

Terminology: imagery

Zoomorphism

A type of imagery where a person, object or entity is described as having characteristics of an animal.

E.g.: "Bob clawed his way through the undergrowth in search of his lost car keys."

"The leaves were swept in a windblown gallop across the lawn."

Hyperbole

Imagery which uses powerful exaggeration.

E.g.: "I ruined my crab sandwich by drowning it in mayonnaise."

Terminology: language and structure

Tricolon

Three things listed together. Tricolons are common in persuasive language. It's a better term for "the power of three".

E.g.: "To succeed in life you need guts, determination and optimism!"

"When you are at your very lowest, when you're feeling more pain than you've ever thought possible, when there is no glimpse of hope – that it when you are strongest."

(A tricolon can feature a list of single things, or more complex phrases.)

Anaphora

Common in poetry and drama, but can also occur in prose, anaphora is when consecutive lines start with the same word or phrase. We had an example in Elizabeth Barrett Browning's "How do I love thee?":

> *I love thee freely, as men strive for right.*
> *I love thee purely, as they turn from praise.*
> *I love thee with the passion put to use*

You can comment on the writer's use of anaphora, or the anaphoric structure of writing.

Epistrophe

This is the opposite of anaphora – when lines end with the same word/phrase.

Hyperbaton

A useful term for a sentence with a convoluted syntax (which means a mixed up order of words).

E.g.: "some rise by sin, and some by virtue fall".

The natural syntax here would be "fall by virtue". The hyperbaton is used to put greater emphasis on what causes the "fall".

Tautology

A tautology is a phrase composed of two or more words that mean the same thing. Generally considered bad style, but writers sometimes use tautology for emphatic effect.

Earlier in the "Jane Eyre" extract, Jane describes John with the tautology "wicked and cruel boy".

At the time of writing, a commonly heard tautology is "global pandemic". "Pandemic" means an illness with global spread, so "global" is unnecessary to add in this phrase.

Tautology/tautological. Also known as "pleonasm".

Polysyndeton and asyndeton

A polysyndeton is a list in which each item is separated by "and". E.g.: to make the best crab sandwich you need fresh crab and fresh bred and mayonnaise and crispy lettuce and lemon juice.

An asyndeton is where there are no "and"s separating the items in the list.

They are useful to comment on, because they can affect the pace, the intensity, or the tone of whatever's being described.

Prolepsis and analepsis

Very similar to foreshadowing, a prolepsis is a moment in a story that links to something which happens later in the story. Conversely, an analepsis is a moment that links to something which already happened earlier in the story.

Aposiopesis

Common in dialogue, an aposiopesis is an unfinished bit of speech.

A common example: "You better do what you're told, or else."

Although it ends with a full stop, the idea isn't complete. Or else what? The consequence is left implied.

It can be useful to comment on, because it's often used when characters can't bring themselves to say something uncomfortable, or to imply a threat rather than give it directly.

Don't confuse aposiopesis with interruption, where a second character stops the speaker from talking. Aposiopesis is where the speaker chooses to leave the sentence incomplete.

Litotes

Litotes is a specific form of understatement, where two negatives are used to make a positive statement. Example:

Well, that crab sandwich <u>wasn't</u> the <u>worst</u> I've ever eaten."

The two negatives are underlined. Together they make a positive statement – the sandwich was okay, it was acceptable – but it's understatement. It leaves the impression that the sandwich really wasn't anything great.

Elizabeth Bishop's poem "One Art", which comes up in the IGCSE syllabus, features heavy use of litotes. The speaker claims "the art of losing isn't hard to master". The speaker is trying to say that it's easy to learn how to lose things and not get upset by losing things, but the litotes leaves us unconvinced, and implies that in fact she is greatly troubled by the things she has lost.

EMERGENCY TERMS

So called because they are really useful when you want to comment on language, but you can't find any specific device in the quotation to analyse.

Connotation

"Connotation" means "association". We can write about the connotations of the word a writer uses, and how it shapes effect.

For example, imagine we're writing about a poem which has the word "black" in the first line. What are the connotations (associations) of this word? Sadness? Death? Despair? That sort of thing – which leads to good analysis of how the writer is shaping the mood at the start of the poem.

How to use it in a sentence:

The word "black" has connotations of despair / the word "black" connotes despair.

Diction

The writer's diction is the writer's specific choice of individual words. Take for example this quotation:

"He clutched at his briefcase".

It's not a great one for analysis – there's no imagery. But we can comment on the diction of "clutched", and how the writer uses it to give a sense of the character's desperation.

Diction is really useful to comment on in otherwise uninteresting quotations.

Tone

The tone of a piece of writing means the mood, or feeling, that is created. Look at this quotation from the start of Charles Dickens' "Great Expectations" and think about what sort of tone the writer shapes:

At such a time I found out for certain that this bleak place overgrown with nettles was the churchyard; and that Philip Pirrip, late of this parish, and also Georgiana wife of the above, were dead and buried; and that Alexander, Bartholomew, Abraham, Tobias, and Roger, infant children of the aforesaid, were also dead and buried.

We could do some lovely analysis on the diction of "bleak", and the references to the "churchyard" and death, and how they shape a foreboding tone.

Connotation, diction and tone can be used in analyses of pretty much any quotation, so keep them up your sleeve but don't rely solely on them. The best essays use a good range of analytical approaches.

TECHNIQUES

Strategies for integrating quotations

Integrating quotations skilfully is one of the best things you can do to strengthen the overall impression of your essay. I've touched on this before, but a reminder of what integrating means:

When you are commenting on a quotation from the text, you should blend the quotation into the sentence you are writing so that it becomes a grammatical component of your sentence.

Look how integration can really help the flow of your writing:

NOT INTEGRATED: *The speaker says the lady is more lovely and more temperate than a summer's day. "Thou art more lovely and more temperate".*

INTEGRATED: *The speaker says the lady is "more lovely and more temperate" than a summer's day.*

Using parentheses can help integrate quotations, e.g.:

The speaker uses positive diction ("lovely" and "temperate") in his comparison.

When you need to change something in the original quotation so it makes sense in your integration, use square brackets:

The speaker says "[she] is more lovely and temperate".

(The original quotation is "thou" instead of "she".)

If you're integrating a long quotation, trim out bits you don't need with an ellipsis (...):

The speaker's belief that "so long as men can breathe...this gives life to thee" serves to immortalise the lady in the poem.

CARPing

Another technique I've mentioned before, but so important it gets a second mention. CARPing is something you SHOULDN'T do. NOT doing it can have a massive improvement on the analytical focus of your writing. Unfortunately, a lot of candidates do it by default. CARPing means writing about

Characters

As

Real

People.

For an example, let's take this comment on the character of Eddie from Arthur Miller's "A View from the Bridge":

Eddie often makes himself a victim, shown by phrases such as "I'm a patsy" and "I walked hungry".

It's CARPing. It shows no awareness that Eddie is a construct shaped by a writer. As often as possible, we want to avoid CARPing, which we do by putting focus on the writer instead of the character. This is easy to do. Just start with the writer:

Miller characterises Eddie as someone who sees himself to be a victim, shown by phrases such as "I'm a patsy" and "I walked hungry".

Suddenly it comes across as much more analytical and much less descriptive. It makes a massive difference.

Occasional moments of CARPing are okay. If you look back at the example essays in this book, you'll see some CARPy comments. Starting every analytical sentence with the writer's name would get a bit clunky. But across your main paragraph, the focus should mainly be on the writer.

FREQUENT ERRORS

We all make mistakes, and we all have own favourite mistakes that we make quite often. Looking back over your essays and your teacher's marking is the best way to correct your own common mistakes, but I'll mention a couple of frequently occurring ones here.

Imply and infer

These two words are very easy to mix up, but they mean different things.

A reader infers. "Infer" means to "interpret", which is something only a reader can do. A text cannot infer.

NICE: From this language the reader can infer that Geoffrey is not a very nice person...

NOT NICE: This language infers that Geoffrey is not a nice person.

For the second sentence, we want "implies" instead of "infers". "To imply" means to give an impression; to hint at an idea. It's something texts do, not readers.

The two words are very frequently mixed up in essays; using them correctly stands out to examiners.

Although and whereas

These two very common words are lethally dangerous. They should be left alone unless you're sure you know how to use them correctly!

The reason they're so often misused is because of how we talk. In everyday speech, they've both come to be used in ways that aren't grammatically correct.

This shouldn't necessarily be a big deal, except it really stands out when they're used wrongly.

They should both be used in complex sentences where one idea is being contrasted against another, e.g.:

Although Macbeth's not a very nice character he does have some redeeming features.

Or:

Macbeth's not a very nice character, although he does have some redeeming features.

Notice – it's one sentence with 'although' used to draw a contrast between two ideas in the same sentence.

In everyday speech, the word "although" has been misused so we get sentences like this:

Macbeth's not a very nice character. Although, he does have some redeeming features.

Ouch. It doesn't look good to examiners. Here, "although" is being used in a sentence with only one idea. Wrong!

"Whereas" is misused in the same way. It's a bit more difficult to use correctly.

It must also be used in a sentence contrasting opposing ideas, but for two separate entities. Therefore it wouldn't work in the sentence above:

WRONG: Macbeth's not a very nice character, whereas he does have some redeeming features.

It doesn't work because there's only one entity in the sentence: Macbeth. We need two entities:

CORRECT: Macbeth isn't a very nice character, whereas Banquo is nice.

Or:

Whereas Macbeth isn't a very nice character, Banquo is nice.

It's worth remembering that examiners aren't looking to punish grammatical slips. Their main interest is in your ideas, your analyses, your engagement. But if you're shooting for the highest marks, it is important to get the accuracy of your writing as strong as possible – otherwise the overall impression of your essay's strength is compromised.

Reader/audience; play/poem/novel

When you must write essays on poems and on drama and on novels (notice the nice polysyndeton there) it can be really easy to mix these words up, but remember:

When writing about a play, refer to the audience – not the reader.

When writing about a novel or poem, refer to the reader.

Incorrect formatting of titles

This is something else that stands out to examiners and can damage the overall impression of your answer. Make sure to use quotation marks and capitals when writing the title of the text:

NO: John Steinbeck's novel of mice and men is about two men called George and Lennie...

YES: John Steinbeck's novel "Of Mice and Men" is about two men called George and Lennie...

FINAL WORDS

Literature essays are all about showing off your skill. Yes, some knowledge is required – you've got to have knowledge of the texts you've studied in class. But your skill in thinking of ideas, of responding to language, is so much more important. Just as the singer must rely on skill when on stage, and the basketball player must rely on skill on the court, you must rely on your skill in the exam – you have to rely on yourself. Don't let yourself down. Be confident. Have faith in yourself. You're clever; you've got good ideas. I can tell from here! Good luck out there folks.

EXAMPLE ANSWERS

Here are the example essays used earlier in the book printed in their entirety.

DRAMA/WHOLE TEXT: To what extent do you believe Macbeth is a powerful character?

On the face of it, I'd certainly argue that Macbeth, the eponymous protagonist of Shakespeare's play, is a powerful character. His rise from 'valiant' soldier to King of Scotland is a quick and violent one, and sees him shedding the blood of his best friend, the rightful king, and innocent women and children. His power is unquestionable in its tyranny – but not in its morality. I believe Shakespeare is showing us the discrepancy between two types of power – martial power, and the power of the moral conscience. It is the latter where Macbeth seems much weaker, and much more susceptible to the influence of external forces.

Shakespeare portrays Macbeth's martial power – the character begins as a brave soldier and becomes an unrelenting tyrant. Shakespeare establishes Macbeth's power early; when the sergeant reports on the battle against Macdonwald in 1.2, he describes Macbeth's 'brandished steel...which smoked with bloody execution' on the battlefield. The metaphor of Macbeth's sword 'smoking' with mists of blood creates an undeniably powerful impression of the character quite literally tearing through his enemies. It strikes me as quite horrific, but Shakespeare's diction of 'execution' brings a sense of justice to Macbeth's martial power – his enemies, just like criminals, are being justly executed rather than murdered. The metonym of 'steel' shapes impressions of power through its connotations of hardness and danger, attributes which are transferred to Macbeth himself. Overall, there's quite a hyperbolic tone – it seems to me as if Macbeth is being elevated to a figure from myth, an effect compounded by Shakespeare's choice to have this description narrated by the sergeant. The audience is hearing the legend of Macbeth, not the reality, which already brings into question just how real and reliable his power actually is. Shakespeare gives another demonstration of Macbeth's strength as the character prepares for the murder of King Duncan in Act 2. At the end of his famous 'dagger' monologue, Macbeth seems to build a powerful confidence, as shown in his declarative statements such as 'I go, and [the murder] is done'. He seems fully committed to the act. However, I think Shakespeare again casts some ambiguity about the true extent of Macbeth's power. When the character says 'the bell invites me', it gives me the impression that Macbeth isn't acting entirely of his own agency, but is being coerced by external forces (the 'bell'). Later, when Macbeth himself takes the throne from the murdered Duncan, initially he strikes a powerful figure – symbolised by the grand banquet held for the Scottish nobility. Shakespeare shows Macbeth commanding his lords to 'sit down' and adopting spoken mannerisms of royalty such as the plural pronoun: 'our self will mingle with society'. But this outward show of strength is immediately undone when he begins hallucinating Banquo's ghost. Therefore, while Shakespeare does portray Macbeth as possessing martial power, it is a power that is constantly undermined. I think Shakespeare is showing the audience that martial 'power' held by tyrants is something quite superficial, and is often nothing more than a performance to hide the tyrant's weaknesses.

Shakespeare raises further issues about the superficiality of power by showing how Macbeth's is heavily undermined by external forces such as his wife and the witches. I find it striking how Shakespeare is very quick to undermine the audience's initial impressions of Macbeth's martial power, which starts to happen in the first few scenes. In act one scene five, Lady Macbeth reads his letter about the witches' prophecy that he will become king. In a soliloquy, she worries that he is "too full of the milk of human kindness" to "catch the nearest way" (meaning to kill the current king and take his place on the throne). Shakespeare plays on the feminine, maternal connotations of "milk" to strip Macbeth of his masculine power. "Too full" implies an unsettling idea that "power" and "kindness" are mutually exclusive. She goes on to wish for Macbeth's return home, so she can "pour [her] spirits in [his] ear" – she plans to exert her own power of persuasion on him. In this metaphorical imagery, Shakespeare makes Macbeth become a mere object, something like a jug that can have liquid "poured" into it. This is a sharp way of conveying Macbeth's lack of power – he is passive rather than active; influenced rather than influencing. I think Shakespeare's staging is really important here. Lady Macbeth is alone on stage and Macbeth is absent, which gives a strong visual cue about who holds power in the relationship. The witches, another feminine entity, also serve to strip Macbeth of power. Banquo describes Macbeth as "rapt" when they first see the witches on the "heath", as if Macbeth is immediately subject to their

115

control. When he visits them again in act four scene one, the witches' power over Macbeth, and his lack of power, is again highlighted by Shakespeare. The witches' conjuring of apparitions such as the "bloody child", the "show of eight kings" etc. feels remarkably theatrical, as if the audience is watching a play within a play. To me it feels orchestrated and contrived, but Macbeth fails to register this and takes the witches in good faith. Shakespeare crafts strong dramatic irony, where the audience can see Macbeth is being tricked but he cannot. In that sense, the audience have more power than Macbeth. Therefore, I think Shakespeare shows us how fragile "power" can be. Macbeth's outward appearance of being powerful is completely undermined by the influence exerted upon him by Lady Macbeth and the witches.

There is something else Shakespeare does which makes me feel the protagonist is not powerful: he makes Macbeth become an immoral character, and gives power to the more moral Scottish rebels whom Macbeth battles against at the end of the play. In defeating Macbeth, the rebels take his martial power, but their moral power is what leads the audience to celebrate their victory and align with them. Shakespeare's structuring of the final act gives me a strong sense of how the rebels' morality juxtaposes, and highlights, Macbeth's lack of morality. The scenes alternate strictly between the rebels and Macbeth. In those with the rebels, we see Malcolm, the rightful king, speaking with compassion and comradeship: "cousins, I hope the days are near at hand that chambers will be safe...I would the friends we miss were safe arrived". He addresses the soldiers he commands as family, rather than by their lower status, and Shakespeare gives him diction that connotes moral integrity such as "safe" and "friends". This juxtaposes sharply with Macbeth's scenes, where calls his servant a "cream-faced loon" and commands him to "go prick thy face". His language lacks moral integrity, being characterised instead by crude, monosyllabic fury. This later manifests in Macbeth's actions as well as his language. When Young Siward bravely confronts the "abhorred tyrant", Macbeth shows no mercy, striking him down with a "smile" and "laugh". Shakespeare's showing the horrified audience a lot about power, here. Whilst Macbeth still has the power of physical force, it has no value without the power of morality. Shakespeare rams this home when Macbeth loses his physical, martial power – emblematised by the image of righteous Macduff exiting the stage "with Macbeth's (dead) body".

To conclude, I believe Shakespeare shows us a Macbeth who is powerful in a martial sense, but not powerful on more profound levels, such as moral strength. I find it interesting how true power in the play comes from sources such as the female (Lady Macbeth and the witches) and compassion (Malcolm), which is particularly surprising considering the era in which the play was written. I think Shakespeare was challenging the norms and expectations his audience would have been familiar with.

POETRY

HOW DO I LOVE THEE? Elizabeth Barrett Browning

How do I love thee? Let me count the ways.
I love thee to the depth and breadth and height
My soul can reach, when feeling out of sight
For the ends of being and ideal grace.
I love thee to the level of every day's
Most quiet need, by sun and candle-light.
I love thee freely, as men strive for right.
I love thee purely, as they turn from praise.
I love thee with the passion put to use
In my old griefs, and with my childhood's faith.
I love thee with a love I seemed to lose
With my lost saints. I love thee with the breath,
Smiles, tears, of all my life; and, if God choose,
I shall but love thee better after death.

EXAM QUESTION: How does Browning portray interesting ideas about love in this poem?

Browning's poem features a speaker who seems to be addressing a lover. The poem focuses on the speaker's description of the love she feels and explores the complexities of love as a concept. It's possible the speaker is based on Browning herself, as she had a passionate romance and marriage with Robert Browning, another Victorian-era poet. I find it really fascinating how the poem treats love in complex ways that you wouldn't necessarily expect in a conventional, stereotypical romantic poem. Browning explores how love can be both passionate and gentle, and how it can edify the person who experiences it. I feel Browning intends to show how "love" is

117

something more than just an emotion; instead, it is a powerful force that can change people.

The idea that love is more than a mere emotion becomes apparent at the start of the poem, where the speaker claims to love the addressee to a "depth and breadth and height". Browning uses this tricolon of physical diction to give the sense that love has actual physical dimension. It gives me the impression that love has a tangible presence and a weighty force, an unexpected and interesting idea about love, and it's emphasised by the simple monosyllabic and polysyndetic structure of the image. I really like the way this forcefulness of love is developed when the speaker compares her feeling of love to every day's most "quiet need". This is an oxymoron, where "quiet" conveys the tranquillity love brings while "need" suggests the urgency and strength of the feeling. Part of what makes the poem so interesting is the pace, and Browning quickly moves on to compare love with profound concepts such as justice ("men strive for right") and modesty ("they turn from praise"). I think this quick pace, enhanced by the anaphoric repetition of "I love thee", really conveys the interesting complexity and intensity of love. This complexity is developed with another tricolon toward the poem's end, where Browning attributes love to "breath, smiles, tears" – I really like the intensity created by the asyndetic structure here. "Smiles" and "tears" clearly connote the broad emotional spectrum of love, while "breath" conveys something about the sheer vitality of love – it is as vital an experience to life as the process of breathing. The poem's concluding idea is remarkably interesting – the speaker's declaration that she will "love thee better after death" suggests the ultimate power of love is something that can outlast the physical human body and exist beyond the death of that body. I think Browning is keen to show how the concept of love is far greater than its conventional portrayal as a strong emotion – it is something that has real force and power, perhaps second only to "God".

I think Browning's choice of form is interesting, and important for the poem's point of exploring unexpected ideas about love. Browning chooses the sonnet form, which ostensibly is conventional as sonnets traditionally focus on love. But it's interesting how Browning uses the Petrarchan sonnet form, which is older than the Shakespearean sonnet. I think she does this to create irony – she uses the most traditional sonnet form to explore love in untraditional ways. Browning follows quite strictly the conventional rhyme scheme of the form, which leads to some interesting pairings. "Height", "sight" and "light" emphasise the idea about love being a tangible force, whereas "faith" and "breath", an intriguing half rhyme, alludes to the other extreme – that love is something beyond the physical, but is profound and vital. The rhythm is mainly regular iambic pentameter, which helps the sense of love as reliable and permanent, but has some interesting irregularities. There are spondaic stresses in "breath, smiles, tears" and the repeated "love thee" that break the rhythm but draw attention to the forcefulness of love. Overall, I think Browning's choice and use of form is clever and ironically highlights how love is more interesting and complex than it is traditionally portrayed.

Browning's handling of the poem's structure is also important for how she portrays the interesting complexity of love. As is conventional for the Petrarchan sonnet form, the poem has a volta between the octave and the sestet. After the octave focuses on describing the experience of love ("free", "pure", "ideal grace") the sestet shifts focus onto the edifying nature of love. I think it's really interesting how Browning implies love can "put to use" the "passion" of "old grief", as if love can repair darker emotions. The sestet feels particularly personal and intimate, with lots of syntax putting focus on the speaker's self and the relationship with the addressee ("I love thee with a love"). The reference to the speaker's "lost saints" could allude to the siblings Browning lost at a young age, adding to the fascinating personal intensity of the poem. It's interesting how Browning chooses to use a first-person speaker, as it really highlights how love impacts and changes the person who feels it – I think this is conveyed more powerfully than a third-person perspective would allow.

To conclude, what makes the ideas about love in the poem so interesting is that they go beyond the traditional portrayal of love as a romantic concept. Browning shows how love is more than just a feeling, but a force that is as vital to life as breathing. It is both comforting and fiercely passionate. I really like how Browning portrays love as something that can repair – it feeds on our "grief" to give us something that can even last after death.

PROSE/EXTRACT: "Jane Eyre"

> "What were you doing behind the curtain?" he asked.
> "I was reading."
> "Show the book."

I returned to the window and fetched it thence.

"You have no business to take our books; you are a dependent, mama says; you have no money; your father left you none; you ought to beg, and not to live here with gentlemen's children like us, and eat the same meals we do, and wear clothes at our mama's expense. Now, I'll teach you to rummage my bookshelves: for they are mine; all the house belongs to me, or will do in a few years. Go and stand by the door, out of the way of the mirror and the windows."

I did so, not at first aware what was his intention; but when I saw him lift and poise the book and stand in act to hurl it, I instinctively started aside with a cry of alarm: not soon enough, however; the volume was flung, it hit me, and I fell, striking my head against the door and cutting it. The cut bled, the pain was sharp: my terror had passed its climax; other feelings succeeded.

"Wicked and cruel boy!" I said. "You are like a murderer—you are like a slave-driver—you are like the Roman emperors!"

I had read Goldsmith's History of Rome, and had formed my opinion of Nero, Caligula, etc. Also I had drawn parallels in silence, which I never thought thus to have declared aloud.

"What! what!" he cried. "Did she say that to me? Did you hear her, Eliza and Georgiana? Won't I tell mama? but first—"

He ran headlong at me: I felt him grasp my hair and my shoulder: he had closed with a desperate thing. I really saw in him a tyrant, a murderer. I felt a drop or two of blood from my head trickle down my neck, and was sensible of somewhat pungent suffering: these sensations for the time predominated over fear, and I received him in frantic sort. I don't very well know what I did with my hands, but he called me "Rat! Rat!" and bellowed out aloud. Aid was near him: Eliza and Georgiana had run for Mrs. Reed, who was gone upstairs: she now came upon the scene, followed by Bessie and her maid Abbot. We were parted: I heard the words—

"Dear! dear! What a fury to fly at Master John!"

"Did ever anybody see such a picture of passion!"

Then Mrs. Reed subjoined—

"Take her away to the red-room, and lock her in there." Four hands were immediately laid upon me, and I was borne upstairs

QUESTION: How does Brontë's writing make you sympathise with Jane's character in this extract?

This extract comes toward the beginning of the novel, where the young orphan Jane Eyre is living under the guardianship of her aunt Miss Reed. Here, Jane suffers terribly at the hands of her cousin John, who abuses her emotionally (by undermining and ostracising her) and physically (by throwing a book at her head). Under instructions of her aunt, Jane is then taken to be locked in the "red room". This moment marks an important stage in the novel's narrative arc, as shortly after this Jane is sent away to Lowood School. But the extract also serves as a foreshadowing of the kind of relationships Jane will have with characters later in the story, particularly Mr Rochester. I think the main way Brontë makes me sympathise with Jane is by making the suffering she goes through quite familiar and relatable, albeit shocking. Jane's autonomy is stripped from her; she acts with integrity despite being treated with none. Brontë is not only foreshadowing what happens to Jane, but is also echoing the type of injustice we see and experience in our own world.

The way Brontë portrays Jane as being stripped of all autonomy makes me feel really sympathetic toward her. Right from the outset, she is subjected to the oppressive interrogatives and imperatives of John, who demands with blunt monosyllabism to know "what were you doing?" and orders her to "show the book". Brontë shapes the crude abruptness of his speech to show how he simply assumes he has the right of control over Jane. I find it upsetting the way Jane tells us "I did so" after being ordered to move by John; the simplicity of the language might make her obedience sound meek, but I think it leads the reader to pity the impossibility of her situation rather than to condemn her of weakness.* There is a moment of triumph in the extract where Jane does act with autonomy, accusing John of being "wicked and cruel", and of being "like a murderer...like a slave driver", after he assaults her. The elegant tautology of "wicked" and "cruel", along with the richness of her similes, juxtaposes with John's crude form of speech and aligns the reader with her – but Brontë is only doing this to really heighten our sympathy when Jane is punished for her autonomy and she is "taken away" to be "locked" in the dreaded red room. Brontë's description of "four hands...laying upon [Jane]" creates great pathos, and the dehumanised "hands" of the oppressing force form a strong visualisation of how Jane is utterly without autonomy. I think this is a really important prolepsis of how Jane's autonomy is threatened by Mr Rochester. She can only ultimately find happiness with him when she goes to him of her own will.

It's not just the profoundly harmful attack on Jane's autonomy that causes me to feel sympathetic; it's also the way Brontë shows how unjustly Jane is treated. She is a good character. There's something deeply upsetting about the situation Brontë contrives: a young girl, Jane, sat quietly by herself, reading a book, suddenly assaulted by a repugnant boy. John is just a little boy, his only power over her is granted by material status that makes him a "gentleman's child" and her a "dependent" who must "beg". The writer portrays Jane as a stoic who quietly endures the abuse in a curiously unemotional way. Apart from brief mention of her "terror passing" and her "cry of alarm", Brontë makes no mention of Jane's emotions. She does not cry. Personally, I think this creates more sympathy in the reader than a character who reacts with emotional outbursts, and it makes John and his outbursts ("he called me 'rat! rat!' and bellowed aloud") seem more immature. Her emotional integrity also contrasts with his brash, aggressive physicality wherein he "runs headlong" at her and "grasps" at her. Brontë develops the integrity of Jane by characterising her intelligence: there's an elevated but not arrogant diction in Jane's speech and thoughts, with words such as "tyrant" and "petulant", which combines with the fact that she uses books to educate herself about "Roman emperors" instead of weaponising them like John. The character's stoicism and intelligence build an integrity that evokes reader sympathy, but also highlights the injustice of the abuse Jane receives.

The strong pathos I feel for Jane is largely due to the way Brontë orchestrates the relationship between the protagonist and reader, and the narrative perspective is a key part of this relationship. Brontë uses Jane's homodiegetic perspective to make us feel closer to the character, as the story is related to us directly through the voice of the character. And it's the close, intimate way it's related that creates such strong sympathy. When Jane acknowledges the "drop or two of blood trickling down [her] neck" and the "sharp pain", it comes across as a private, personal admission of suffering rather than a mere description, and that's because of the perspective Brontë uses. Jane's first-person account reveals important details that a third-person couldn't, such as her "not knowing what she did with [her] hands" when John attacks her. Brontë implies that Jane fights back, but the narrator doesn't acknowledge this, because to do so would risk her seeming prideful. The writer is carefully shaping the reader's relationship with Jane, encouraging admiration of her humility rather than condemnation of her arrogance.

Overall, Brontë is taking great strides to situate Jane's character as a victim of oppression and to align sympathy with us. I think the way Brontë shows how unjustly Jane is treated creates a lot of sympathy, but it's the overwhelming attack on her autonomy that I find most powerful. It's important for the novel as a whole – Jane must find means to exercise autonomy in order to find happiness – but I think Brontë's showing us a lot about the real world, too. The brutal, violent denial of Jane's autonomy is a dramatisation of our own reality. In my opinion, that's what the novel is really about: discovering the power of your own autonomy.

UNSEEN: PROSE EXTRACT

Read carefully the following extract from a novel. In this extract, the narrator (Lockwood) is staying overnight at the house owned by Heathcliff, and receives an unexpected visitor called Catherine Linton.

How does the writer make this moment so memorable for you?

To help you answer this question, you might consider:

- How the writer shapes the atmosphere.
- How the writer portrays Lockwood's reaction to Catherine.
- How the writer portrays Catherine's character.

I heard distinctly the gusty wind, and the driving of the snow; I heard, also, the fir bough repeat its teasing sound, and ascribed it to the right cause: but it annoyed me so much, that I resolved to silence it, if possible; and, I thought, I rose and endeavoured to unhasp the casement. The hook was soldered into the staple: a circumstance observed by me when awake, but forgotten. "I must stop it, nevertheless!" I muttered, knocking my knuckles through the glass, and stretching an arm out to seize the importunate branch; instead of which, my fingers closed on the fingers of a little, ice-cold hand!

The intense horror of nightmare came over me: I tried to draw back my arm, but the hand clung to it, and a most melancholy voice sobbed, "Let me in—let me in!"

"Who are you?" I asked, struggling, meanwhile, to disengage myself.

"Catherine Linton," it replied, shiveringly (why did I think of Linton? I had read Earnshaw twenty times for Linton)—"I'm come home: I'd lost my way on the moor!"

As it spoke, I discerned, obscurely, a child's face looking through the window. Terror made me cruel; and, finding it useless to attempt shaking the creature off, I pulled its wrist on to the broken pane, and rubbed it to and fro till the blood ran down and soaked the bedclothes: still it wailed, "Let me in!" and maintained its tenacious grip, almost maddening me with fear.

"How can I!" I said at length. "Let me go, if you want me to let you in!"

The fingers relaxed, I snatched mine through the hole, hurriedly piled the books up in a pyramid against it, and stopped my ears to exclude the lamentable prayer.

I seemed to keep them closed above a quarter of an hour; yet, the instant I listened again, there was the doleful cry moaning on!

"Begone!" I shouted. "I'll never let you in, not if you beg for twenty years."

"It is twenty years," mourned the voice: "twenty years. I've been a waif for twenty years!"

Thereat began a feeble scratching outside, and the pile of books moved as if thrust forward.

I tried to jump up; but could not stir a limb; and so yelled aloud, in a frenzy of fright.

To my confusion, I discovered the yell was not ideal: hasty footsteps approached my chamber door; somebody pushed it open, with a vigorous hand, and a light glimmered through the squares at the top of the bed. I sat shuddering, yet, and wiping the perspiration from my forehead: the intruder appeared to hesitate, and muttered to himself.

At last, he said, in a half-whisper, plainly not expecting an answer,
"Is any one here?"

I considered it best to confess my presence; for I knew Heathcliff's accents, and feared he might search further, if I kept quiet.

With this intention, I turned and opened the panels. I shall not soon forget the effect my action produced.

Heathcliff stood near the entrance, in his shirt and trousers; with a candle dripping over his fingers, and his face as white as the wall behind him. The first creak of the oak startled him like an electric shock: the light *leaped from his hold to a distance of some feet, and his agitation was so extreme, that he could hardly pick it up.*

"It is only your guest, sir," I called out, desirous to spare him the humiliation of exposing his cowardice further. "I had the misfortune to scream in my sleep, owing to a frightful nightmare. I'm sorry I disturbed you."

(waif = homeless child)

On the surface, this extract is certainly a memorable moment due to the very unusual encounter the writer presents between Lockwood and Catherine. The writer gives me the impression that the young girl outside Lockwood's window is in fact a ghost, what with her "doleful moaning" and insistence she's been a "waif for twenty years". But there's much ambiguity, which only makes it more memorable – the writer suggests at the end that it was nothing more than a "nightmare". Furthermore, the way Heathcliff's character seems so strongly "startled", as if struck by an "electric shock", implies that he may have heard the ghost himself. I feel this extract is about more than a possible ghostly encounter. It's exploring what it's like to be confronted with the unknown. Lockwood is in an unfamiliar, unknown place as a "guest", and is confronted by an unknown entity with an unknown history. The writer shows how the unknown can fling us into turmoil and make us behave in ways unknown to ourselves – as seen with what Lockwood does to Catherine's wrists..

The oppressive pathetic fallacy at the start of the extract immediately helps make the atmosphere memorable. The writer puts heavy emphasis on the forcefulness of the weather outside Lockwood's room with diction such as "gusty" and "driving". Lockwood's repetition of "I heard" when describing the noise of the wind and snow creates unease; it feels as if he is on high alert, for some reason having a heightened awareness. The personification of the fir branch "teasing" against the window makes the atmosphere outside feel more alien and unknown. Lockwood's turmoil when confronted with the unknown is highlighted by his remarkably drastic action of "knocking [his] knuckles through the glass" in order to silence the branch. When he realises he's holding someone's hand instead of the branch, I think the writer is turning a familiar situation (touching another person) into something really alarming and uncomfortable, which the sharp description of the "ice-cold" hand achieves. This builds a memorably uneasy, alien atmosphere which persists throughout the encounter and remains afterwards, when Heathcliff finds Lockwood. I think here the writer draws our attention to the possibility that there's something amiss with Heathcliff's reaction – he doesn't notice the hot candle wax "dripping over his fingers", and his face is as "white as the wall". It makes me feel that Heathcliff knows something about Catherine, but because the story is related to us through the first-person narration of Lockwood, it remains unknown to the reader. The writer gives me a really strong sense of how disorientating it is to be confronted with the unknown.

Initially, the writer's use of ambiguity makes Lockwood's reaction to Catherine memorable. Although the encounter is not framed as if it is taking place in the narrator's sleep, when the girl grasps Lockwood's hand it is the "intense horror of nightmare" that he feels. Is it real or not? The writer keeps us confounded by the unknown. The writer builds on Lockwood's reaction of horror, describing how he "tried to draw back [his] arm but the hand clung to it', straightforward diction giving a clear and unsettling implication of the girl's supernatural strength. When the girl speaks her name, the narrator questions "why did I think of Linton?" as if he himself decided the name in a dream, which makes me feel even more disorientated. The writer describes how "terror made [Lockwood] feel cruel" when he sees Catherine's face, which seems to me an incongruous reaction to seeing a little girl, but the aggression of the word "cruel" shows how strong an impact this unknown situation has on Lockwood. It's an impact the writer makes extremely shocking and memorable when Lockwood proceeds to "pull its wrist on the broken pane, and rub it to and fro, until blood dripped down". Suddenly there's no ambiguity – the language is very clear, heightening the shock felt by the reader at Lockwood's reaction. The dehumanising use of "its" instead of "her" again shows how Lockwood is transformed by the unknown into something uncompassionate. When Lockwood declares "I'll never let you in, not if you beg for twenty years", I think the writer uses the cruelty of his tone to show how fear can transform a person. Overall, Lockwood's reaction is a memorable demonstration by the writer of how the fear of the unknown so severely impacts us.

The way Catherine's portrayed by the writer is a big part of what makes this extract so memorable for me, and the narrative perspective plays an important role in this. Although the reader would naturally align with the first-person narrator, who's inevitably the closest character to the reader, I find myself distanced from Lockwood due to his response to the girl and sympathise more with Catherine. Her "doleful moaning", which continues incessantly in the form of a "lamentable prayer" even after Lockwood has waited fifteen minutes for it to silence, makes heavy use of emotive diction that is both pitiable and ominous. Her simplistic, repetitive phrases of "let me in!" and "twenty years!" make her seem familiarly childlike yet we can't escape the implication of her supernatural presence. The writer is making her seem simultaneously familiar and unsettlingly unknown. The writer further highlights her familiar childishness with the slightly ungrammatical speech of "I'm come home; I'd lost my way" – but how can she have been lost for twenty years? She is disarmingly pitiable but is also an assault on our rationality. When Lockwood must listen to her "feeble scratching" outside his window, I'm torn between feeling sympathy for Lockwood and pity for her weakness conveyed by "feeble". The writer's structuring is impactful – Catherine is a dominating presence throughout the extract until suddenly she's gone: Heathcliff's "hasty footsteps" arrive and there's no more mention of the girl. It makes me think there's some sort of unknown relationship between Heathcliff and her, as if they can't exist in the same space.

In conclusion, this extract provides on the surface a very memorable encounter between a man and a ghostly entity. But it's the writer's deeper ideas about being confronted with the unknown that I personally find truly memorable. The writer shows how the fear of something unknown has such terrible influence on Lockwood. Further than this, the reader is given a direct sense of being in conflict with the unknown: we're not sure whether to sympathise with Lockwood or be appalled by him; we're not sure whether Catherine is a pitiable young "waif" or a terrifying, inhuman "creature". We're not even sure whether the encounter happens in reality. Furthermore, it seems to me that all three characters are somewhat lonely. They are separated by different realms of existence or different layers of knowledge. The writer gives me such a strong sense of the isolating and disorientating impact of the unknown on us.

Printed in Great Britain
by Amazon

17498530R00078